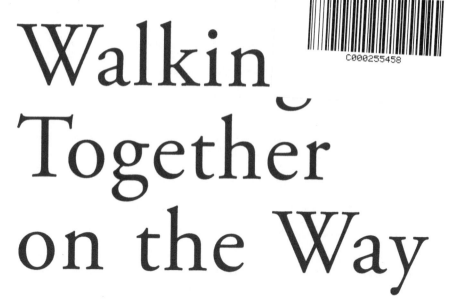

Walking Together on the Way

Learning to Be the Church— Local, Regional, Universal

An Agreed Statement of the Third Anglican– Roman Catholic International Commission (ARCIC III)

Erfurt 2017

First published in Great Britain in 2018

Society for Promoting Christian Knowledge
36 Causton Street
London SW1P 4ST
www.spck.org.uk

British Library Cataloguing-in-Publication Data
A catalogue record for this book is available from the British Library

ISBN 978-0-281-07894-3
eBook ISBN 978-0-281-07878-3

Typeset by Fakenham Prepress Solutions, Fakenham, Norfolk NR21 8NL
First printed in Great Britain by Ashford Colour Press

eBook by Fakenham Prepress Solutions, Fakenham, Norfolk NR21 8NL

Produced on paper from sustainable forests

Contents

Abbreviations

AA	Second Vatican Council, *Apostolicam Actuositatem*. Decree on the Apostolate of the Laity (1965)
ACC	Anglican Consultative Council
AL	Pope Francis, *Amoris Lætitia*. Post-Synodal Apostolic Exhortation on Love in the Family (2016)
ARCIC	Anglican–Roman Catholic International Commission
AS	Pope John Paul II, *Apostolos Suos*. Apostolic Letter issued 'Motu Proprio' on the Theological and Juridical Nature of Episcopal Conferences (1998)
Auth I	ARCIC I, *Authority in the Church I* (Venice, 1976)
Auth I Elucidation	ARCIC I, *Authority in the Church I: Elucidation* (Windsor, 1981)
Auth II	ARCIC I, *Authority in the Church II* (Windsor, 1981)
CaC	ARCIC II, *Church as Communion* (1991)
CCEO	Pope John Paul II, *Codex Canonum Ecclesiarum Orientalium*. The Code of Canons of the Eastern Churches (1990)
CD	Second Vatican Council, *Christus Dominus*. Decree Concerning the Pastoral Office of Bishops in the Church (1965)
CFL	Pope John Paul II, *Christifideles Laici*. Apostolic Exhortation on the Vocation and the Mission of the Lay Faithful in the Church and the World (1988)
CIC	Pope John Paul II, *Codex Iuris Canonici*. The Code of Canon Law of the Catholic Church (1983)
CN	Congregation for the Doctrine of the Faith, *Communionis Notio*. Letter to the Bishops of the Catholic Church on some Aspects of the Church Understood as Communion (1992)
ED	ARCIC I, *Eucharistic Doctrine* (1971)
EE	Pope John Paul II, *Ecclesia de Eucharistia*. Encyclical Letter on the Eucharist in Its Relationship to the Church (2003)

EG	Pope Francis, *Evangelii Gaudium*. Apostolic Exhortation on the Proclamation of the Gospel in Today's World (2013)
EV	Pope John Paul II, *Evangelium Vitae*. Encyclical Letter on the Value and Inviolability of Human Life (1995)
Gift	ARCIC II, *The Gift of Authority (Authority in the Church III)* (1999)
GTUM	IARCCUM, *Growing Together in Unity and Mission: Building on 40 Years of Anglican – Roman Catholic Dialogue* (2007)
IARCCUM	International Anglican–Roman Catholic Commission for Unity and Mission
IASCUFO *Report*	The Inter-Anglican Standing Commission on Unity, Faith and Order, *Report to ACC-15* (2012)
LC	Lambeth Conference (followed by date)
LG	Second Vatican Council, *Lumen Gentium*. The Dogmatic Constitution on the Church (1964)
LiC	ARCIC II, *Life in Christ: Morals, Communion and the Church* (1994)
Mary	ARCIC II, *Mary: Grace and Hope in Christ* (2005)
MIDI	Pope Francis, *Mitis Iudex Dominus Iesus*. Apostolic Letter 'Motu Proprio' by which the Canons of the Code of Canon Law Pertaining to Cases Regarding the Nullity of Marriage are Reformed (2015)
MO	ARCIC I, *Ministry and Ordination* (1973)
OA	Pope Paul VI, *Octogesima Adveniens*. Apostolic Letter on the Occasion of the Eightieth Anniversary of the Encyclical *Rerum Novarum* (1971)
OS	Pope John Paul II, *Ordinatio Sacerdotalis*. Apostolic Letter on Reserving Priestly Ordination to Men Alone (1994)
PCL	*Principles of Canon Law Common to the Churches of the Anglican Communion* (2008)
PO	Second Vatican Council, *Presbyterorum Ordinis*. Decree on the Ministry and Life of Priests (1965)
S&C	ARCIC II, *Salvation and the Church* (1987)
SC	Second Vatican Council, *Sacrosanctum Concilium*. Constitution on the Sacred Liturgy (1963)
SFLC	International Theological Commission, *Sensus Fidei in the Life of the Church* (2014)

TCTCV	World Council of Churches, *The Church: Towards a Common Vision*. Faith and Order Paper No. 214 (Geneva: WCC Publications, 2013)
TSI	The Inter-Anglican Standing Commission on Unity, Faith and Order, *Towards a Symphony of Instruments: A Historical and Theological Consideration of the Instruments of Communion of the Anglican Communion* (2015)
TT	International Theological Commission, *Theology Today: Perspectives, Principles, and Criteria* (2011)
UR	Second Vatican Council, *Unitatis Redintegratio*. Decree on Ecumenism (1964)
UUS	Pope John Paul II, *Ut Unum Sint*. Encyclical on Commitment to Ecumenism (1995)
VR	*The Virginia Report of the Inter-Anglican Theological and Doctrinal Commission* (1997)
WCC	World Council of Churches
WR	The Lambeth Commission on Communion, *The Windsor Report* (2004)
WT	IARCCUM, *Walking Together: Common Service to the World and Witness to the Gospel* (2016)

Usage of Terms

In their respective documents Anglicans and Roman Catholics sometimes use the same terms in different ways. For both precision and ease of comprehension the Commission here explains its use of the following terms.

Bishop of Rome
: In this, as in previous ARCIC Agreed Statements, the Pope, variously referred to as the Supreme Pontiff, the Servant of the Servants of God, the Holy Father, and other historic titles, is normally styled Bishop of Rome. It is because the particular church of Rome is where both Saints Peter and Paul laboured and were martyred that the See of Rome and its bishop, *successor Petri*, enjoy a pre-eminent authority and honour in the universal Church.

Catholics
: While recognizing that the term 'catholic' is used by a wide variety of Christian traditions, the Commission uses 'Catholics' to refer to all who are in full communion with the Bishop of Rome, recognizing that Eastern Rite Catholics (as above) would not self-describe as *Roman* Catholics.

Church catholic
: The Commission uses 'Church catholic' in reference to the one Church of Christ.

Deliberative
: In this statement 'to deliberate' connotes 'to discuss and debate'; 'deliberative' denotes 'authorized to reach a decision'. 'Deliberative' thus means that a particular body, e.g. a synod, can decide a matter of policy by an authoritative vote.

Eastern Catholic Churches
: There are twenty-three Eastern Catholic Churches that are in full communion with the Bishop of Rome. Together they constitute just over 1 per cent, or 16 million, of the faithful of the Catholic Church. With the exception of the Maronite Church, all these churches have come into full communion with the Bishop of Rome since the sixteenth century; however, they have retained their liturgical rites, which they share in common with the Eastern

and Oriental Orthodox churches from which they originate. They are headed by patriarchs, major archbishops, and metropolitans and are governed by the Code of Canons of the Eastern Churches (1990), though each has its own Canon Law in addition to this Code.

Instruments of communion The Commission uses 'instruments of communion' to refer in this document to respective Anglican and Roman Catholic structures, procedures, and ministries which serve to maintain the quality and reality of communion at the local, regional, and worldwide levels of Anglican and Roman Catholic life. Although the term has roots in particular Anglican usage, the Commission has adopted the term with broader reference to both traditions.

Latin Church This is by far the largest of the churches of the communion of the Catholic Church, and in the strict sense is what is meant by the 'Roman Catholic Church'. The vast majority of Catholics globally belong to it. In origin it is the Church that spread throughout the Roman Empire, and whose common language was Latin. It is governed by the Code of Canon Law (*Codex Iuris Canonici*) published in 1983.

Local church For the sake of clarity and following previous ARCIC usage (e.g. *Auth I* §8; *Gift* §13), throughout this document 'local church' will routinely refer to the diocesan church, or its equivalent, headed by a bishop.

Receptive learning Receptive learning is that process whereby each of our traditions asks itself whether instruments of communion and other elements of church life found in the other tradition might suggest a way of furthering the mission of the church in one's own tradition. 'Receptive learning' does not presume that elements from one tradition can usually be directly borrowed from the other. One tradition might decide that, in some cases, some processes or instruments in another tradition would not be suitable. But the term suggests a positive openness to study and evaluation of what seems to work in another tradition, with a view to adapting it to one's own. Receptive learning is the way in which ARCIC III has appropriated the approach of receptive ecumenism.

Regional level In this document 'regional levels of ecclesial life' will be used to refer to the trans-local ecclesial bodies respectively corresponding with Anglican provincial churches and groupings of churches overseen by Roman Catholic episcopal conferences.

Roman Catholic Church The Commission follows previous ARCIC usage and the title of the Commission in using 'Roman Catholic Church' to refer to all the churches, East and West, which are in full communion with the Bishop of Rome. In doing so, the Commission recognizes that Eastern Catholics do not describe themselves as 'Roman'; even within the Latin rite the prefix 'Roman' has fallen out of common usage in the years since the Second Vatican Council.

Trans-local The Commission uses 'trans-local' to refer to any expression of church life beyond the level of the diocese: that is to say, at the metropolitan, regional, national, and worldwide levels.

Universal/ worldwide church Anglicans understand themselves to be *part* of the one Church of Christ, while Roman Catholic doctrine makes the claim that the one Church of Christ *subsists* in the Roman Catholic Church (*LG* §8). These differences in self-understanding mean that there are differences in the ways in which we speak of the church as a global reality. Catholics frequently use the term 'universal church' to speak of the total communion of particular diocesan churches around the world in full communion with the Bishop of Rome. Anglicans typically understand 'universal church' to refer to the one Church of Christ through time and space—the mystical body of Christ—and to all Christian communities in real but impaired communion throughout the world. Anglicans do not use 'universal church' as a synonym for the existing Anglican Communion, for which the 'worldwide

Anglican Communion', or 'the global Anglican Communion', is the preferred term. In this document 'universal church' and 'worldwide communion' will each be used, as context and sense require.

Preface

By the Co-Chairs of ARCIC III

After centuries of living apart, the Anglican Communion and the Roman Catholic Church have been on pilgrimage together since the historic visit of Archbishop Michael Ramsey to Pope Paul VI in March 1966. The establishment of the Anglican–Roman Catholic International Commission (ARCIC), now in its third major phase of work, grew out of that visit as a tangible expression of the joint commitment to walk together the path of ecclesial conversion and renewal so that, as traditions, we might grow into the fullness of communion in Christ and the Spirit.

Two interrelated themes have had an abiding presence in the work of ARCIC since its inception in 1970: the question of authority and the ecclesiology of communion. This current document takes up these two themes again, and seeks to develop them in a new way. In doing so the Commission is responding to the 2006 Common Declaration of Pope Benedict and Archbishop Williams, which identified two critical areas for our future ecumenical dialogue: 'the emerging ecclesiological and ethical factors making that journey more difficult and arduous'. Reflecting this, the Commission has been asked to examine 'the Church as Communion, local and universal, and how in communion the local and universal Church come to discern right ethical teaching'. Our current document addresses the first of these two themes.

Both of our traditions affirm that ecclesial communion is rooted in Word, sacrament, common creedal faith, and the episcopate (Lambeth Quadrilateral, from LC 1888, Resolution 11; and *CN* §11). Ecclesial communion requires that the structures and procedures which serve and express the bonds of communion are attended to with diligence and care. This document examines how well these instruments of communion serve us and maintain the unity in diversity that communion implies. This task requires frank assessment: the courage to look at ourselves honestly and to learn from the other. It is a task that resonates with Pope Francis's call for a fully synodal Church in accord with the vision of the Second Vatican Council,[1] while Anglicans continue to explore the meaning and efficacy of synodality for its life in communion at all levels.

---

[1] Pope Francis, 'Address Commemorating the 50th Anniversary of the Institution of the Synod of Bishops' (17 October 2015).

It is our hope that *Walking Together on the Way: Learning to Be the Church—Local, Regional, Universal* will be a part of this ongoing process of honest self-reflection and growth. In their 2016 Common Declaration, Pope Francis and Archbishop Justin Welby declared: 'While, like our predecessors, we ourselves do not yet see solutions to the obstacles before us, we are undeterred. In our trust and joy in the Holy Spirit we are confident that dialogue and engagement with one another will deepen our understanding and help us to discern the mind of Christ for his Church.'

It is important to make clear that by 'together' the Commission envisages each communion attending to its own structures and instruments, but aided by the support and example provided by the other communion. The sense is of our two traditions each walking the pilgrim way in each other's company: 'pilgrim companions,'[2] making their own journey of conversion into greater life but supported by the other as they do so. At times the Commission has chosen to represent this by presenting our respective Anglican and Roman Catholic analyses of our structures and their challenges in parallel columns. This allows us to recognize the similar but differentiated ways in which our respective structures seek to serve our communions. At other times, in order to avoid appearing to equate quite different processes, we use a sequential format, but with those paragraphs on the left-hand side of the page in an Anglican voice, and those on the right-hand side in a Roman Catholic voice. This side by side analysis of our structures allows us to identify what is challenged, what is graced, and what we may have to learn from our dialogue partner or pilgrim companion. The conviction is that by examining and reforming our respective instruments of communion alongside and in conversation with each other, we are also growing closer to each other and strengthening the imperfect communion that already exists between us.

When discussing our respective structures and their challenges at the local (Section IV), regional (Section V), and worldwide (Section VI) levels of our respective ecclesial lives, in each case the discussion moves through three phases: first, describing what currently is the case for each of our traditions at the level in view; second, identifying what respective tensions and difficulties are experienced at this level; and third, in relation

---

[2] Archbishop Justin Welby and Pope Francis, 'Commissioning the IARCCUM Bishops' (5 October 2016), San Gregorio al Celio, Rome; also the IARCCUM Bishops begin their statement: 'As shepherds of Christ's flock we have come together from nineteen regions of the world, representing our churches, to take steps together as Anglicans and Roman Catholics along the pilgrimage to a common life and mission. We rejoice in the many fruits of our ecumenical journey so far' (*WT*).

to these tensions and difficulties, asking what possibilities there might be for transformative receptive learning from the other tradition. This task requires frank assessment, repentance, and the courage to look at ourselves honestly and learn from the other.

The work of ARCIC I and ARCIC II shows how the Commission has developed a range of Agreed Statements in response to its mandate, which have varied in length, style, method, structure, and intention. ARCIC III hopes that its fresh approach, chosen in response to its mandate, will enable and equip Anglicans and Catholics to learn from one another and grow together in fidelity to Christ's will for the Church.

This Agreed Statement was concluded in Erfurt, Germany, where Martin Luther studied, took his vows as an Augustinian friar, was ordained, and taught before being called to Wittenberg in 1511. The Commission was privileged to undertake its work in Erfurt, under the hospitality of the Bildunghaus St Ursula, during the 500th anniversary of the Reformation, signalling the contribution of this dialogue to the wider ecumenical journey.

As Co-Chairs we are delighted to present this Agreed Statement to our respective authorities and the faithful of both of our traditions, in the sincere hope that our dialogue can contribute to the flourishing of each of our communions, both by modelling how such mutual learning can today be pursued and by acting as a means of grace through which each communion is more perfectly configured to the image of Christ. This task is always before the Church *semper reformanda*.

+ Bernard Longley
+ David Moxon
Erfurt, Germany, 2017

The Status of the Document

The document published here is the work of the Anglican–Roman Catholic International Commission. It is a joint statement of the Commission. The authorities who appointed the Commission have allowed the statement to be published so that it may be widely discussed. It is not an authoritative declaration by the Roman Catholic Church or by the Anglican Communion, which will evaluate the document in order to take a position on it in due time.

Citations from Scripture are from the New Revised Standard Version.

I. Introduction

The goal of the dialogue: visible unity and full ecclesial communion

1. The goal of the Anglican–Roman Catholic dialogue, established in 1966 during the visit of Archbishop Michael Ramsey to Pope Paul VI, has been successively reiterated by subsequent Popes and Archbishops of Canterbury in the series of Common Declarations issued at particularly important meetings together. This goal, always recognized as a gift rather than a human product, has been succinctly expressed as:

   the restoration of complete communion in faith and sacramental life

   and

   visible unity and full ecclesial communion.

   As Pope Francis and Archbishop Justin said in their Common Declaration of 2016, current differences and obstacles to unity 'cannot prevent us from recognizing one another as brothers and sisters in Christ by reason of our common baptism. Nor should they ever hold us back from discovering and rejoicing in the deep Christian faith and holiness we find within each other's traditions. These differences must not lead to a lessening of our ecumenical endeavours.'

Résumé of ARCIC Statements so far

2. Towards this goal successive Anglican–Roman Catholic International Commissions have offered their respective traditions a series of Agreed Statements and related resources on issues which have divided Anglicans and Catholics in the past and still do today:[1]

---

[1] For a summary, see *GTUM*, pp. 2–30. For the Agreed Statements of ARCIC I (*The Final Report*), together with related documents, see Christopher Hill and Edward Yarnold (eds.), *Anglicans and Roman Catholics: The Search for Unity* (London: SPCK/CTS, 1994). For the Agreed Statements of ARCIC II, as well as supporting essays, see Adelbert Denaux, Nicholas Sagovsky, and Charles Sherlock (eds.), *Looking Towards a Church Fully Reconciled: The Final Report of the Anglican–Roman Catholic International Commission 1983–2005 (ARCIC II)* (London: SPCK, 2016). ARCIC II also issued *Clarifications of Certain Aspects of the Agreed Statements on Eucharist and Ministry of the First Anglican–Roman Catholic International Commission* (London: CTS/Church House, 1994).

ARCIC I

1971 *Eucharistic Doctrine*
1973 *Ministry and Ordination*
1976 *Authority in the Church I*
1979 Elucidation of *Eucharistic Doctrine*
1979 Elucidation of *Ministry*
1981 *Authority in the Church I Elucidation*
1981 *Authority in the Church II*

ARCIC II

1987 *Salvation and the Church*
1991 *Church as Communion*
1994 *Life in Christ: Morals, Communion and the Church*
1999 *The Gift of Authority (Authority in the Church III)*
2005 *Mary: Grace and Hope in Christ*

Many of these agreements have been in part or whole received with appropriate criticism by the authorities of the two communions. Some of the work of ARCIC, especially its work on the meaning of communion, which is profoundly relevant for the work of the present Commission, has been incorporated into wider ecumenical thinking.

Communion and communion ecclesiology for Catholics and Anglicans

3. Together with the emphasis on the Church as the pilgrim People of God, an understanding of the Church as communion (*koinonia*) has been immensely important in Roman Catholic ecclesiology since the Second Vatican Council. Here the twin streams of renewal, of returning to the great sources of the tradition (*ressourcement*) and engaging the issues of our age (*aggiornamento*), together with the impact of ecumenical dialogue, have all been in evidence. Similarly, the churches of the Anglican Communion have also been exploring the deeper meaning of communion that arises from their engagement with one another (see *VR*) and in ecumenical dialogue, particularly through ARCIC, the Anglican–Orthodox dialogue, and the Anglican–Lutheran dialogue, and through their participation in the Faith and Order Commission of the WCC. This exploration of the nature of communion has become vital in the light of current debates within the churches.

Summary of ARCIC work so far on authority

4. Also of particular significance for the current work of the Commission has been the successive progress made in *Authority in the Church I* (1976), *Authority in the Church II* (1981), and *The Gift of Authority* (1999). Where *Authority in the Church I* reached a high degree of agreement on 'the basic principles of primacy', *Authority in the Church II* examined persisting differences concerning papal authority. In turn, *The Gift of Authority* called for a possible ecumenical role for the Bishop of Rome even in the current structurally divided state of Christianity. It identified difficulties which Anglicans and Catholics continue to find in the other's characteristic way of relating the local and the universal to each other. When ARCIC II looked at the Anglican Communion, its questions concerned the apparent lack of an ecclesial 'centre' (*Gift* §56). When it looked at the Roman Catholic Church, its questions concerned the proper roles of the local and provincial churches—and in particular the role of the laity—in ecclesial decision-making (*Gift* §57).

The distance still to be travelled

5. However, despite these significant achievements and fifty years of formal commitment to seeking unity, ARCIC recognizes that the distance to be travelled is considerably greater than the optimism of the early days suggested. As Popes and Archbishops of Canterbury have successively and unequivocally recommitted Anglicans and Catholics to the goal of unity, with increasing clarity and frankness they have also noted that new obstacles have arisen. The ordination of women to the presbyterate and episcopate, together with decisions by some Anglican churches in relation to matters of human sexuality, have raised serious questions for the Roman Catholic Church about the dispersed nature of the structures of authority within the Anglican Communion (*LiC* §54). From the Anglican perspective, some critics have questioned the desirability of pursuing the stated goal of unity with the Roman Catholic Church on the grounds of a perceived centralization of authority as well as anxiety about limitations on the decision-making roles of the laity. The establishment of personal ordinariates, equivalent in Latin Catholic canon law to dioceses, for those Anglicans who as groups have left Anglican churches to enter into full communion with the Roman Catholic

Church, is seen as further reason for caution by some members of the Anglican Communion. Other Anglicans have accepted this development as a pastoral response which should not be seen as overturning the long-term goal of ARCIC. Despite such serious questioning and criticism, neither the Anglican Communion nor the Roman Catholic Church has deviated from their commitment to the goal of visible unity.

Post-Reformation differences: the impact of mission

6. Other disagreements and differences have developed since the separation of our communions. During the centuries after the Reformation our traditions developed different cultures, with patterns and practices of authority that diverged from each other. The ministry of the Church of England spread across the world with the expansion of British commerce and Empire. With the new-found independence of the Protestant Episcopal Church of the USA and the emergence of self-governing churches, much indebted to the work of missionary societies, in the longer-established colonies new regional structures of authority were developed within a growing Anglican Communion. These local ecclesial identities and regional histories lie at the root of the diversity within the Anglican Communion today. The Roman Catholic Church expanded in similar fashion, as a result of the work of missionary orders and the support of colonial powers. This growth also led to the need, in newly planted missions and churches, for structures of authority which respected both their local identity and their being members of the universal Church. In both cases, our traditions are dealing with the effects of colonization particularly in relation to indigenous peoples and their cultures. The Anglican and Roman Catholic traditions have thus, in separation, to a significant degree developed distinctive structures of authority in response to similar experiences and problems in mission.

Contemporary global contexts

7. Christian churches now live in a new globalizing age, where societies worldwide are undergoing rapid and radical change. Previously accepted forms of historical understanding, which gave access to overarching perspectives expressing ancient wisdom, are in many places giving way to limited or private narratives and disconnected meanings. This raises major issues for Christian faith

and living: fragmented approaches to the Scriptures and Christian tradition undermine the preaching of the Gospel and life in communion. In the West, generations are growing up with world-views shaped by secular presuppositions and the immediacy of electronic communication. There is increasing uncertainty about the value of its Christian heritage. For younger churches in other parts of the world, the priority is to attend to urgent and practical tasks: they have few resources to develop local institutions of Christian learning and formation. Given this new global context, the tasks of engaging with cultures, religions, and stark social inequalities take new forms. Anglicans and Catholics alike need to develop local and trans-local structures which enable them to draw closer to one another as they engage with the challenges of a new age.

New areas of collaboration and mission

8. Alongside fresh obstacles must be set the welcome emergence of new areas of collaboration and mission, for example, at the international level, common action in opposition to modern slavery and human trafficking, and at the national level, in some parts of the world, increased episcopal trust and collaboration on matters of social justice, together with the articulation of a common voice in the public square. This was symbolized on 5 October 2016, when Archbishop Justin Welby and Pope Francis jointly commissioned nineteen pairs of Anglican and Catholic bishops from Asia, the South Pacific, Africa, Europe, and the Americas to work together in ecumenical mission and witness. The bishops, who were meeting in Canterbury and Rome as the International Anglican–Roman Catholic Commission for Unity and Mission (IARCCUM), subsequently published a short statement about their meeting in which they wrote, 'In these days we have … listened with immense joy to testimonies of profound friendship. We have heard stories of common witness and mission where existing ecumenical directives are being applied creatively and faithfully with great practical effectiveness at the service of the kingdom of God' (*WT*). Similarly, ARCIC III has usually met in locations where Anglicans and Catholics collaborate.

Significant internal cultural differences within and across our separate communions

9.   In addition, both traditions are also increasingly aware of highly significant internal cultural differences *within* and *across* our separate communions. English or 'Anglo-Saxon' culture is no longer the primary carrier of Anglican faith and worship throughout the global Anglican Communion. Nor is European culture for the worldwide Roman Catholic Church. Here, Anglicans and Catholics must learn together about the rich diversity of communion: the Church more truly catholic, more truly universal in space and in time.

Issues raised about the relationship between local churches and the universal Church

10.   After the conclusion of the work of ARCIC II in 2005, the dialogue was not immediately resumed. The constitution of a new Commission (ARCIC III) and reiteration of the original goal in 2011 are indicative both of long-term confidence in the search for Anglican–Roman Catholic unity and of commitment to addressing, with charity and frankness, the more recent obstacles that have emerged. These recent obstacles raise issues about the relationship between the local and regional levels of church life on the one hand, and the worldwide level on the other hand.[2] They specifically raise questions as to how contentious matters of decision-making and discernment of right ethical teaching are handled across these levels. In this context the Commission's mandate, in two parts, has required it to explore some of the central questions dividing us and common challenges facing us by charging ARCIC III to explore: 'The Church as Communion, local and universal, and how in communion the local and universal Church come to discern right ethical teaching.'

Why we have decided to study the regional alongside local and universal levels of ecclesial life

11.   The ARCIC mandate specifies 'the Church as communion, local and universal', but in both our traditions there are instruments of communion among the local churches that exist not only globally

---

[2]   In this document, common ecumenical practice is followed by speaking of *levels* with respect to the structures that sustain the life of the Church, whether local or trans-local.

but regionally. The Anglican Communion is composed of provincial churches consisting of many dioceses. In some areas smaller groupings of dioceses, such as metropolitical provinces, are to be found. The Catholic Church organizes dioceses, or their equivalents, into regions largely marked by national boundaries, served by an episcopal conference or a patriarchate. On a smaller scale, it organizes dioceses into metropolitan areas and provinces, potentially comprising a number of metropolitan areas.

Regional instruments of communion have existed in the Church almost from its beginning so that church authorities can promote consistency in pastoral life and cohesion in doctrine. In antiquity regional synods were the customary occasions for consecrating bishops, reviewing discipline, and debating doctrine. Some regional synods of antiquity proved to be enormously influential in shaping the faith of the universal Church (e.g. Elvira 306) or in provoking debate at the universal level (e.g. Toledo 589). The importance of the *regional* in the life of the Church is stressed in the 2007 Ravenna Statement of the Joint International Commission for the Theological Dialogue between the Roman Catholic Church and the Orthodox Church.

The utility of the regional bodies is evident: the churches of a given culture are well served when the authorities of several local churches make decisions in concert with one another; the churches of a region help keep any local church from straying from communion; and the life of the church in a region can give witness to the universal Church concerning aspects of the inexhaustible riches of Christ that are a common treasure. For these reasons, the Commission has decided, in line with other ecumenical dialogues, to consider various regional instruments of communion as well as those pertaining to the Church local and universal.

The value of controversy, debate, dialogue, and synodal processes

12. Dialogue within our respective traditions about such difficult matters as the proper place for decisions on questions of ministry and human sexuality should be welcomed rather than feared. At all times in the Church, from its earliest days to the present, controversy, debate, dialogue, and synodal processes have led—eventually and often not quickly—to clarification and ultimately a more precise articulation of 'the faith that was once for all entrusted to the saints' (Jude 1.3). A classic example is the eventual resolution of the

Arian controversy at and after the Council of Nicaea of 325, from which in due time emerged a profound and distinctively Christian articulation of the divinity of Christ and the salvific reality of the Incarnation. The development of doctrine shows that contested questions, often debated vigorously throughout the Church, locally, regionally, and globally, can lead eventually to a deeper common understanding and more precise articulation of the truth.

The focus of ARCIC III in this document

13. This first Agreed Statement of ARCIC III focuses on the first half of the Commission's mandate: on the relationship between the local and the universal in the Church as communion. Recognizing that we begin both with a history of fragmentation *between* our traditions and with tensions *within* them, this document addresses questions which arise as we consider how our respective traditions engage in decision-making at local and trans-local levels, and how we each discern the appropriate level for particular decisions.

This Agreed Statement prepares the ground for the second document of the Commission

14. Although the primary focus in this Agreed Statement is on the ecclesiological dimension of the Commission's mandate, the study of respective structures and processes of decision-making is also of relevance for the second part of our mandate, concerning discernment of right ethical teaching. Accordingly, this first Statement paves the way for a second document which will engage with the ethical aspect of the mandate in a sustained and explicit fashion. While this Statement focuses on 'structures and processes' we acknowledge that there are many other sources of influence on the shaping of church teaching, such as the tradition, the work of theologians, the lives and writings of the saints, and responses of Christians to societal evils.

The Commission's method: both continuity and development

15. In working to fulfil both parts of its mandate, ARCIC III recognizes both continuity and development of its method from its two predecessors. ARCIC I discerned a level of agreement by looking behind past polemics and the different but complementary ways of speaking that developed after separation. ARCIC II deepened this approach in *Church as Communion* (1991) by emphasizing,

as the title of this Agreed Statement indicates, that dialogue is a matter of growing more deeply together in the Trinitarian communion of God. In *Life in Christ* (1994), it was acknowledged that while some areas of disagreement cannot be wholly overcome, they could be re-evaluated as not justifying division. Following the 1989 Common Declaration of Archbishop Robert Runcie and Pope John Paul II, ARCIC III recognizes that 'the ecumenical journey is not only about the removal of obstacles but also about the sharing of gifts'. This implies more than ceasing to judge the other tradition as mistaken or problematic but discerning in what ways it is graced and, therefore, offers certain distinctive gifts that can be gratefully received. As Pope John Paul II stated: 'Dialogue is not simply an exchange of ideas. In some way it is always an "exchange of gifts"' (*UUS* §28; the reference is to *LG* §13).

Building on *The Gift of Authority* and *Mary: Grace and Hope in Christ*

16. In this ARCIC III builds upon and develops the emphasis in earlier ARCIC work on the need to learn how to recognize and receive the ecclesial presence of Christ in the other. In *The Gift of Authority* (1999) and *Mary: Grace and Hope in Christ* (2005), ARCIC II considered issues that have emerged since our separation. In these, the Commission argued that a view of tradition that focuses on how issues have been articulated in the past is inadequate. Developing the concept of 're-reception' (*Gift* §§24–25), it employed a method which focuses on how divisive issues can be approached afresh by considering them from God's future 'backwards' (see *Mary* §§52–53). This 'eschatological' method is reflected in the title of the final report of ARCIC II, *Looking Towards a Church Fully Reconciled* (2016).

The importance of self-critique

17. Building on all of the above and recognizing: (i) the development in separation of the two traditions, (ii) the current serious obstacles to full communion, and (iii) the internal difficulties faced by each tradition, ARCIC III believes that the time is ripe to pursue the task of ecumenical engagement as one that includes explicit ecclesial self-critique. It is not enough to recognize that there is something of gift and grace in the other. We must explore what God has given to our partners which, as Pope Francis has said, 'is also meant to be a gift for us' (*EG* §246). This is particularly so when such 'treasure[s]

to be shared' (*Anglicanorum Coetibus*, §III) address difficulties in one's own tradition.[3]

The method of receptive ecumenism

18. This process involves being prepared both to discern what appears to be overlooked or underdeveloped in one's own tradition and to ask whether such things are better developed in the other tradition. It then requires the openness to ask how such perceived strengths in the other tradition might be able, through receptive learning, to help with the development and enrichment of this aspect of ecclesial life within one's own tradition. This method, commonly called receptive ecumenism,[4] is an approach which is strongly influenced by Pope John Paul II's request of church leaders and theologians from other traditions to help reimagine the practice of papacy (*UUS* §§95–96). It is deeply resonant with the respective teachings of Pope Francis (*EG* §246, cited above) and Archbishop Justin Welby. Preaching at Westminster Abbey in 2016 when celebrating fifty years of the Anglican Centre in Rome, the Archbishop said: 'The habits of the centuries render us comfortable with disunity ... I pray that ARCIC disrupts our disunity ... it must develop its especial genius of a spirit of receptive ecumenism: of asking not what we might give the other, but what we lack that God might give us through the other.'

Receptive learning as a source for renewal for our ecclesial lives

19. ARCIC III is convinced that, just as a return to the sources of tradition in Scripture, liturgy, and the Patristic and Scholastic periods (*ressourcement*) has been renewing both Anglican and Roman Catholic theology since the middle of the last century, so critical self-examination through the prism of ecumenical dialogue and

---

3   Pope Francis, 'General Audience' (22 January 2014): 'It is good to acknowledge the grace with which God blesses us and, even more so, to find in other Christians something of which we are in need, something that we can receive as a gift from our brothers and our sisters.' In *EG* §246 he gives a specific example: '[I]n the dialogue with our Orthodox brothers and sisters, we Catholics have the opportunity to learn more about the meaning of episcopal collegiality and their experience of synodality.'

4   The essential principle in receptive ecumenism is that in the context of mature dialogues, the current moment requires primary emphasis to be placed on what one's own tradition needs to learn from the partner, rather than the other way around: see Paul D. Murray (ed.), *Receptive Ecumenism and the Call to Catholic Learning: Exploring a Way for Contemporary Ecumenism*. For ARCIC III's adoption of receptive ecumenism as key to its method, see the communiqué arising from the Commission's first meeting in May 2011 at Bose, Italy.

receptive learning can deepen the renewal and participation of the Church in the Trinitarian communion of God.

The four sections of the document

20. Following an opening biblical reflection on the Church local and universal (Section II), this document is developed in four main sections. The first of these (Section III) sets out the fundamentals of a theology of ecclesial communion by focusing on the ecclesial implications of baptism and eucharist. The necessary interrelationship of the local and the trans-local is here explored, as too is the need for effective instruments of communion. This section finishes by stating the need both to recognize the limits and difficulties associated with respective instruments of communion and to examine the possibility of their transformation through receptive ecumenical learning. The following three sections (Sections IV, V, and VI) deal in turn with the structures of local churches, various regional instruments of communion, and the worldwide structures of the Anglican Communion and the Roman Catholic Church. We do this, first, by identifying the structures and processes which are appropriate at the relevant level; second, by identifying any perceived difficulties; and third, by exploring what possibilities there are for fruitful receptive learning across the traditions in these regards.

Walking together into increasing degrees of communion

21. Archbishop Justin Welby and Pope Francis have both used the image of 'walking together' on the path to full communion to describe our ecumenical relations.[5] We are indeed fellow pilgrims journeying at the summons of God's Word, through the difficult terrain of a rapidly changing world. We encounter very similar difficulties along the way, and we struggle to discern what faithful obedience demands. Walking together means that, as travelling companions, we tend each other's wounds, and that we love one another in our woundedness. This journey that we undertake, which is a walking together into increasing degrees of communion *despite* difference, bears powerful and urgent witness to the world as to what it means to live difference well for mutual flourishing.

---

5 See, for example, 'Address of Pope Francis to His Grace Justin Welby, Archbishop of Canterbury and his Entourage,' (16 June 2014). In their 2016 Common Declaration Pope Francis and Archbishop Welby use similar language, writing, 'we have become partners and companions on our pilgrim journey'.

II. The Church Local and Universal in the Apostolic and Post-Apostolic Periods

Introduction

22. The Scriptures do not offer a blueprint as to how we should understand the interconnection between the local and the universal dimension of the Church today. Nevertheless, they offer an orientation and signposts, and indicate some essential aspects of the Church of Christ which are relevant to this understanding. The following section traces the ecclesial patterns to be found in the New Testament and subsequent early Christian history.

Church in the New Testament: local and universal

The *ekklesia* as the gathered People of God

23. Gathering lies at the heart of the notion of 'church'. The Greek word *ekklesia* was widely used in the Hellenistic world to describe a gathering of people and had a clear meaning in the secular context. It is used by many of the New Testament writers to describe the gathered People of God.[6] Some think that this could be a reference to the Septuagint's rendering of the Hebrew word q^{e}hal, or 'assembly'. Whereas *synagoge* was the normal rendering of q^{e}hal, on some occasions it was translated as *ekklesia*. The use of the word, therefore, may have evoked for some of the earliest Christians the notion of Israel as the gathered People of God.

The New Testament use of the term 'church'

24. Many uses of the word 'church' can be found throughout the New Testament (Acts, Matthew, Hebrews, and Revelation). Paul, however, furnishes us with its most extensive range of usage. Sometimes it simply meant an assembly for worship (1 Cor 11.18; 14.19, 34), sometimes a house-congregation (Rom 16.5; Col 4.15; Philem 2), sometimes a distinct local community (e.g. 'the church

---

[6] Mt 16.18; 18.17; widely throughout the Pauline epistles; widely throughout Acts; Jas 5.14; 3 Jn 1.6, 9, 10; and Rev 2.1, 8, 12, 18; 3.1, 7, 14.

of God that is in Corinth' in 1 Cor 1.2 and 2 Cor 1.1; 'the church of Cenchreae' in Rom 16.1; 'the church of the Thessalonians' in 1 Thess 1.1). Sometimes the term (in the plural) points to a larger area with many local churches ('the churches of Galatia' in Gal 1.2; the 'churches of Asia' in 1 Cor 16.19; 'all the churches (of Christ)' in 1 Cor 7.17; Rom 16.16). And lastly, the term is used to indicate the whole body of Christians throughout the world (1 Cor 12.28; 15.9; Gal 1.13; Eph 1.22; Phil 3.6; 1 Tim 3.15).

Local and universal from the beginning

25.   The challenge of the interrelation of the Church local and the Church universal has been implicit for Christian teaching and practice from its beginning. In the Lucan narrative, the Church of Christ started in a specific place, the city of Jerusalem, which was the heart of the Jewish religion, and at the same time a city with a universal horizon, a holy city, a holy mountain for all nations (Isa 2.2–4; Mic 4.1–3). From this account of its origins in Jerusalem, the Church showed a universal openness, because it was commissioned to bring the Gospel of Christ to the whole world. At the outset, however, the universal was experienced in and through the local. For example, in the Matthean account of the resurrection the disciples are told to meet the risen Lord in Galilee of the nations (Mt 28.7, 10).

The *missio Dei*: God wants all human beings to be saved

26.   God 'desires everyone to be saved and to come to the knowledge of the truth' (1 Tim 2.4) through 'the one mediator between God and humankind, Christ Jesus, himself human, who gave himself a ransom for all' (1 Tim 2.5–6). Just as Jesus was sent by the Father for the salvation of the whole world (Jn 3.16–17), so the disciples are sent by the risen Lord to continue his work of salvation (Jn 20.21). The Church is the sacramental manifestation of the *missio Dei* (*CaC* §§16–24). The missionary identity of the Church is universal in scope. The missionary Church can thus be seen to bring to fulfilment the promise once made to Abraham that in him all the tribes of the earth would be blessed (Gen 12.1–3).

The universal commission of the risen Lord in Matthew

27.   In the Gospel of Matthew, the risen Lord commissioned the eleven, locally gathered on the mountain in Galilee, and empowered them with authority to go out and 'make disciples of *all nations*'. Making

disciples has a sacramental and a moral aspect affecting the whole of Christian life. The eleven are commissioned to baptize 'in the name of the Father and of the Son and of the Holy Spirit' (Mt 28.19) and so to initiate the newly baptized into the community of disciples. The eleven are also instructed to teach them 'to obey everything that I have commanded you' (Mt 28.20). Discipleship is a way of life based on the teaching of Jesus; it has to do with both belief and behaviour.

The universal commission of the risen Lord in Luke–Acts

28.   The interrelatedness of the local and the universal dimension of the mission of the disciples is made explicit in Luke–Acts. To the 'eleven gathered together' in Jerusalem, the risen Lord declared that 'repentance and forgiveness of sins is to be proclaimed in his name to all nations, beginning from Jerusalem. You are witnesses of these things' (Lk 24.47–48). Before his ascension, the Lord developed this commission with the phrase: 'you will be my witnesses in Jerusalem, in all Judea and Samaria, and to the ends of the earth' (Acts 1.8). Jesus' command is symbolically fulfilled in the book of Acts, which narrates the mission to Judea and Samaria in chapters 8 and 9 and in which the 'ends of the earth' refers to Rome, not as an end in itself, but as the representative of the whole world, where Paul is allowed to preach the Gospel 'without hindrance' (Acts 28.31).

The local, trans-local, and universal dynamics of the Church in Luke–Acts

29.   Luke shows how the self-designation of 'church' can take a local, trans-local, and even universal meaning. In Luke's account, a definitive moment in the life of the Church occurred in Jerusalem on the day of Pentecost, when the apostles 'were all together in one place' (2.1). In the presence of devout Jews from all nations gathered in Jerusalem (2.5–12), the Holy Spirit was poured out upon all (2.1–4), as was foretold by the prophet Joel in his prophecy concerning the last days (2.14–21), so that the Gospel could be communicable to all nations. As a result of this, some three thousand people were baptized and were added to the initial congregation (2.41; see 4.4: five thousand). Of these, the community that remained in Jerusalem after Pentecost was called 'the church in Jerusalem' (8.1; 11.22). It was, from its earliest days, bilingual (see the 'Hellenists'

and 'Hebrews' in Acts 6) and consisted of several house churches (12.12). It is clear that the 'Church of God', which was fully present in a certain place, could be present at the same time in other places and among other language-groups: together with its local identity, the Church was also a trans-local and universal reality: it was called 'the church [*singular*] throughout Judea, Galilee, and Samaria' (9.31).

30. Furthermore, some refugees from persecution in Jerusalem started a new community in Antioch (Acts 11.19–26), certain members of which also preached the Good News to the Greeks. The church in Antioch (where the disciples were first called Christians) had its own prophets and teachers and, under the guidance of the Spirit, assumed the authority to send out its own missionaries, Barnabas and Saul (13.1-3). This new local church at Antioch in turn generated a family of other local churches.

31. Towards the end of Acts, in Paul's address to the elders of the church in Ephesus, he admonishes them to 'shepherd the church of God that he obtained with the blood of his own Son' (Acts 20.28). Here the phrase 'church of God' points to the local church at Ephesus, but also to the mystery of the Church in its theological and Christological nature (see Col 1.18, 24). Each local church that is in communion with other local churches is the Church of God in that place.

The work and authority of the Holy Spirit

32. In Luke and John, the Holy Spirit was the driving force for the *missio Dei* that led the early Church—the followers of 'the Way' (Acts 9.2)—from Jerusalem, the city of peace for all nations, towards the end of the earth. The Spirit energized and guided events both in the life of Jesus and of the early Church. The Spirit's work revealed the new era and empowered the new community for witness. The Spirit guided the community at key points and made its leaders bold and wise in testimony. The ultimate authority in the *ekklesia* is the Spirit, sent, according to the Fourth Gospel, from the Father and from Christ himself (Jn 15–17), and breathed on the disciples in the Upper Room by the risen Christ (Jn 20.22). In Luke's account, the Spirit was given to the disciples at Pentecost (Acts 2). The Spirit filled the Seven before and at their election (Acts 6). It was the initiative of the Spirit which prompted the admission of Cornelius to the

community by baptism (Acts 10.47). The Holy Spirit was given—after fasting and prayer—by the imposition of hands to Barnabas and Saul for their mission at Antioch (Acts 13:2–4). The Spirit is perceived to be behind the authoritative decision of the community in Jerusalem that Gentile believers do not have to be circumcised (Acts 15:28–29). Every initiative in the young community depicted in Acts was directed by the Spirit.

The emergence of 'instruments of communion'

33. The early Church under the guidance of the Holy Spirit sought to maintain unity while experiencing a growing diversity. For Luke the company of baptized believers was one in heart and soul (Acts 4.32). It lived through disciplined attentiveness to the teaching and fellowship of the apostles, the breaking of the bread, and the prayers (Acts 2.42). Elsewhere in the New Testament, when somebody behaves in clear contradiction to apostolic witness, the local church is entitled to exclude that person from the communion (Mt 18.15–17; Acts 5.1–11; 1 Cor 5.1–5). The 'pillar' apostles (Gal 2.9) represent apostolic authority in the church in Jerusalem. Their authority becomes trans-local when it extends into Judea and Samaria, and even beyond the borders of Palestine (Acts 15; Gal 2). Moreover, some individual apostles do not limit their apostolic activities to Jerusalem but travel around to give testimony to the Gospel in other cities and areas (Acts 8: Philip, Peter, and John in Samaria; Acts 9–10: Peter in Lydda, Joppa, and Caesarea).

34. With the emergence of the church at Antioch and its missionary initiatives among the Gentiles, apostolic authority was not limited to the Twelve but included other apostles (Acts 14.4, 14; Rom 1.1; 1 Cor 1.1; 2 Cor 1.1; Gal 1.1, 15–16). It is now recognized that God causes the Gospel to be communicated along two lines: Peter and the other pillars (James and John) have been entrusted with the Gospel for the circumcised Jews, while Paul and Barnabas have been entrusted with the Gospel for the uncircumcised Gentiles. But this division of the mission and its leadership does not prevent its protagonists from extending to each other the right hand of *koinonia* (Gal 2.7–9), even if this diversity within the churches and the Church sometimes causes tensions and conflicts (Acts 15; 1 Cor 8.1–13; Gal 2.11–15). The apostles become itinerant evangelists. Their corporate authority is both trans-local and universal. It

can be exercised by visits or letters. As can be seen from the many epistles preserved in the canon of the New Testament (and in the early Patristic period), letters were a primary means of maintaining communion among the early Christians. In these epistles the apostles are often seen delegating their authority to local leaders (Acts 11.30; 14.23; 15.2, 4, 6, 22, 23; 16.4; 20.17; 21.18; 1 Tim 5.17, 19; Tit 1.5; Jas 5.14; 1 Pet 5.1).

Decision-making in the early Church

35.   Acts 15 has been understood as a model of how the early Church made decisions and guided the community in Christian living that tried to maintain the unity of the existing communion while at the same time recognizing the growing diversity of the rapidly expanding Church. In the local church of Antioch, as depicted in the Lucan narrative, Greeks were being converted to the Gospel, with the approval of the church at Jerusalem (Acts 11.19ff). Problems arose as to whether these Gentile converts needed to be circumcised and to keep the Law of Moses in order to be baptized as followers of Jesus (Acts 15.1–2). Unable to resolve this question on its own, the church of Antioch sent a delegation (Paul and Barnabas) to consult the church in Jerusalem, implicitly, therefore, recognizing the authority of that church. Luke presents us with an encounter of respectful mutual listening: the leaders of the church in Jerusalem listened to the experiences of representatives of the local church of Antioch, and then the latter listened to the arguments developed by the leaders of the Jerusalem church. The decision taken was under the guidance of the Holy Spirit (15.28), in accord with the Scripture (15.16–18), and involved the whole Church (15.4, 5, 12, 22). The narrative is a programmatic guide to preserving the *koinonia* in a context of dispute. The practice of a local church (Antioch) must be examined and approved by the church that is regarded as the primary guardian of the apostolic tradition (Jerusalem), and this church, in turn, must attend to the pastoral and mission struggles of each particular community. The aim is to achieve, in the power of the Spirit, the unanimity that bears witness to the mind of Christ (*LiC* §§23–26).

Using freedom to care for those weaker in the faith

36.   A similar dynamic can also be found in the Pauline epistles, where on a number of occasions those who are regarded as in some way

'strong' are urged to take care of those whose conscience is weak. In 1 Cor 8.2–13, where the issue at hand was whether members of the Christian community should eat food offered in pagan sacrifices to idols, Paul established the principle of self-restraint out of loving respect and concern for others. Although he, himself, agreed with the 'strong' believers that idols have no power and that food offered to them is no different from any other food, he argued that the freedom they had in Christ dictated that they should take greater care of the 'weak' believers so that they did not stumble in their faith. Such a principle can also be seen in 1 Cor 12.22–23, where greater honour is given to those considered to be less honourable, and in Romans 15.1-3, where the 'strong' are urged to bear the failings of the weak so that they may be built up.

The Jerusalem church and the vision of the New Jerusalem

37. The Jerusalem church occupied an important place in the imagination of the early Church. Paul writes in Galatians of 'the Jerusalem above', saying, 'she is free, and she is our mother' (Gal 4.26). Even after Jerusalem had been destroyed by the Romans, this vision lived on. This vision embodied the reality of the eschatological Church. The idea of a transcendent Jerusalem, in which all earthly churches already share and to which Christians will be admitted when God's purposes are fulfilled, emerges at the conclusion of the book of Revelation (Rev 21.1–14). The book opens with a vision of the Risen Christ holding in his right hand the 'seven stars' which represent the seven churches of Asia Minor, to each of which a letter is addressed (Rev 1.16). The seven churches—of Ephesus, Smyrna, Pergamum, Thyatira, Sardis, Philadelphia, and Laodicea—are also likened to seven golden lampstands, among which Christ walks (2.1). To each is shown a distinctive facet of Christ's glory (2.1; 2.8; 2.12; 2.18; 3.1; 3.7; 3.14). To each is given a distinctive message as to how better to reflect the light of that glory. The need for repentance in these local churches is frequently repeated (2.5; 2.16; 2.22; 3.3; 3.19). In each case, they are encouraged to 'listen to what the Spirit is saying to the churches' (3.22).

Post-apostolic developments

Unity and apostolicity in the context of the Church's growth

38. The Church that emerged from the formative period to which the New Testament bears witness was a Church of the 'one and the

many'. As the Gospel continued to spread, new churches sprang up in an ever-growing diversity of cities and cultures. A continuing concern among the leaders of the churches was the maintenance of unity and fidelity to their apostolic origin. It was recognized that the Gospel could be translated faithfully into new languages (initially, from Greek to Latin) and cultures. But the preaching of the Gospel in new situations raised new questions about the adequacy or inadequacy of what was being said and done: questions about the unity and apostolicity of the Church.

The rule of faith

39. Such concerns are already evident in the New Testament. The concern for faithful transmission of the Gospel can be seen in a wide variety of places in the New Testament itself (see Lk 1.1–4; Jn 2.24; 1 Cor 11.2, 23; 15.3; Gal 1.6–9; 1 Tim 6.3-4; 2 Jn 7) and was maintained in the post-apostolic generations by reference to the body of texts that became the New Testament. It was from what Irenaeus called the 'rule of faith' that the creeds of the Church were developed at the local, the trans-local, and eventually the universal levels.

Questions about the holiness and apostolicity of the Church

40. The consistent practice of baptism, common prayer, the ministry of the Word, and the sharing of the eucharist maintained the life of the Church as a participation in the life of Christ, through the power of the Spirit, but also raised questions about the boundaries of the Church. Questions about who could be baptized or who could share in the eucharist, and who might incur the extreme penalty of exclusion from the eucharist, were already being raised in the New Testament (see Jude 12). These are questions about the holiness and the apostolicity of the Church (Irenaeus, *Adversus Haereses*, 1.10, 1–2).

Bishops and the maintenance of the Church in truth

41. The role of the bishop in maintaining the Church in truth, both by personal example and by faithful teaching, is rooted in the witness of the New Testament (see 1 Tim 1.3–4; 3.1–7; 6.2–4) and emphasized by teachers from the second century, such as Ignatius and Irenaeus. The processes of consultation and discernment, at local and trans-local levels, in the determination to maintain both diversity and

unanimity can be seen in the synodical practice (*Gift* §§34–40) that grew up from the time when the leadership of apostles who had known Jesus historically was no longer available. By the fourth century, bishops, both singly and in collegial unity, came to exercise jurisdiction in the Church. The main concern of the bishops of the post-apostolic Church, at both the local and the trans-local levels, was for the unity, holiness, catholicity, and apostolicity of the whole Church.

The primacy of the Bishop of Rome

42. Over time, the bishops of the patriarchal sees of Rome, Antioch, Alexandria, Constantinople, and Jerusalem assumed wider juridical responsibility at the trans-local level and, in the case of the Bishop of Rome, at the universal level (*Gift* §§45–47). This universal ('Petrine') ministry of the Bishop of Rome was traced back to the apostolic ministry of both Peter and Paul, who witnessed to Christ by their deaths in that city. The importance of the Bishop of Rome among the other bishops was further explained by analogy with the position of Peter among the Twelve as the spokesman, representative disciple, and primary witness of the resurrection (Mt 16.16–19; Mk 16.7; Lk 24.34; 1 Cor 15.5). This primacy was interpreted as Christ's will and continues to be significant for the Church (see *Auth I* §§11–12). Already in the First Epistle of Clement (late first century), the Bishop of Rome can be seen giving guidance to uphold the unity of the Corinthian church against divisive teaching.

Regional and ecumenical councils

43. From the early days of the Church, bishops began to gather together to consult about matters of importance. Regional synods were from time to time convoked by metropolitans and patriarchs. These were largely clerical gatherings, but lay people, especially from among monastic delegations, did sometimes participate. There are records of many such synods from the second century. Not until the fourth century was there a synod which was intended to be ecumenical. The Council of Nicaea (325) was convoked by the Emperor Constantine to settle the dispute over the teaching of Arius which was then dividing the Church. Its teaching was widely received throughout the Church of East and West. The Creed which the Council affirmed was received and developed by later councils as a trustworthy statement of the Christian faith. The canons promulgated by councils

were a growing resource to guide the Church on a wide range of issues.

The reception of the decision of councils

44.   The importance of the reception of council decisions for local Christian churches can be traced back to the Lucan account of the reception of the letter from the Jerusalem church to the church of Antioch, after the deliberations of the Jerusalem church over the necessity of circumcision for baptism. When the Antiochene Christians received the letter, setting out the minimal requirements for participation in the life of the Church, which did not include circumcision, 'they rejoiced at the exhortation' (Acts 15.31). In the same way, controversial questions in the life of the churches were later remitted to regional, and eventually ecumenical, councils. Deliberation took place at the councils, in the confidence that the Spirit would guide the participants and in the hope of achieving unanimity. The teaching of councils was received because it reflected the faith as it was already practised by the local churches, guiding and developing their Christian life to a fuller and clearer expression. The authority of conciliar teaching came not only from the representative authority of the council that delivered it, whether regional or ecumenical, but also from the perceived authenticity of the teaching itself.

A diverse pattern of ministry

45.   Despite sharp and vigorous disagreements about the requirement for circumcision and observance of the Jewish law (see Gal 1–2; Acts 15), the need for Christian unity and apostolicity (see Jude 3) was seen to be paramount. The emerging picture in the apostolic and post-apostolic churches is of a pluralist model of witness and authority according to the needs arising from its expansion, both local and trans-local. This diverse pattern of ministry took various forms, including those which quickly became identifiable as episcopal and diaconal, and presbyteral ministries. As local, regional, and universal church structures emerged, it was the bishops who carried authority, in communion with one another and with all the churches, at each level. Presbyters and deacons exercised their specific duties primarily within the local churches. It is with these scriptural orientations, and the development of instruments of communion within the early Church in mind, that we now turn to the teaching and practice of the Church today.

III. Ecclesial Communion in Christ: The Need for Effective Instruments of Communion

Local and trans-local dimensions of ecclesial life in Anglican and Roman Catholic understanding

46. Christ actively incorporates men and women into his body in baptism. Christ's grace moves us to repent of sin, including the sin of division. It heals our wounds, and calls us to eschatological communion, anticipated in eucharistic communion. Our participation (*koinonia*) in Christ leads to tangible means of responding to Christ's call, namely structures that promote life in the fellowship (*koinonia*) of the Holy Spirit (*CaC* §§15, 45–46). Structures of themselves are more limited than the life of grace, just as language is often more limited than the reality it seeks to communicate.

    The following main sections (IV–VI) focus on the relationship between the local and the trans-local dimensions of ecclesial life. They explore structures within our respective traditions and reflect on what each might fruitfully learn from the other. Anglicans and Catholics have some differing understandings, practices, and structures, as well as differences of vocabulary (see 'Usage of Terms'). The aim here is not to eradicate these differences. The point rather is to ask how each might be a resource for the other so that what is experienced as grace and benefit in one might help address what is less developed in the other.

The autonomy and interrelatedness of the local church

47. There are also highly significant aspects of church life which each of our traditions affirms, albeit with characteristically differing emphases. Specifically, each in its own way affirms a fullness of ecclesial reality and relative autonomy at the level of diocese gathered around its bishop.[7] Each also affirms the need for the interrelatedness of local churches at the various trans-local levels of

---

[7] *Auth I* §8. *Lumen Gentium* describes bishops as 'vicars and ambassadors of Christ' and continues that they are not 'to be regarded as vicars of the Roman Pontiffs, for they exercise an authority that is proper to them, and are quite correctly called "prelates". heads of the people whom they govern' (§27).

province, nation, region, and worldwide communion in a manner beyond a federal association (see *Gift* §37).

The dangers of an over-emphasis on autonomy

48. Moreover, Anglicans and Catholics each affirm and experience, albeit asymmetrically, that these two poles, local and trans-local, exist in a certain tension with each other. Too strong an emphasis on local autonomy risks straining important ecclesial bonds at the trans-local level. This potentially leads to insufficient critical distance from the prevailing culture and inadequate attention to the expressions and practice of faith in other parts of the Church. If a diocesan church or regional/provincial structure does not actively participate in this mission beyond its own borders and immediate concerns, it can lose awareness of a vital dimension of its identity within the universal mission of God.

The dangers of an over-emphasis on the trans-local

49. Equally, too strong an emphasis on the trans-local risks the Church becoming overly centralized in a manner that hinders appropriate local adaptation for the sake of mission. This can lead to the proclamation of a Gospel that does not properly enter into specific cultural realities.

50. Mindful of this shared tension, the following sections of this Agreed Statement explore the differing specific instruments of communion within and between the local and trans-local levels of Anglican and Roman Catholic ecclesial life and ask how each tradition might learn from the other. The current section explores further our shared understanding of ecclesial existence, local and trans-local, as these have been identified in previous rounds of ARCIC and other related intra-confessional and ecumenical dialogues. The focus in this section is on the ecclesial implications of baptism and eucharist in Anglican and Roman Catholic understanding.

Baptized into the communion of saints

Baptism as an incorporation into the body of Christ

51. In response to Jesus' commission to 'make disciples of all nations, baptizing them in the name of the Father and of the Son and of the Holy Spirit' (Mt 28.19), both Anglicans and Catholics view baptism as incorporation into the body of Christ. It immerses the baptized

in the stream of an ecclesial existence that is at once local in focus, but also trans-local and universal. Throughout it is eschatological in orientation and implication. Each Christian is initiated into participation in the life of the risen Christ in the Spirit (Rom 6.3–4) in a specific river, pool, baptistery, or font in a particular place, with a particular local community of faith, support, and sponsorship (usually a parish), and into a particular web of relationships.

What it means to be one of the baptized

52. All the baptized are initiated into the *tria munera Christi*, that is, the threefold office and mission of Christ as *prophet, priest,* and *king,* and each is called to an active sharing in that ministry.[8] Each of the baptized shares in Christ's role as *prophet,* because baptism makes one receptive to the Word of God, and the Spirit of truth impels the baptized to share the Good News (Rom 8:14–15). Similarly, each shares in the ministry of Christ as *priest* inasmuch as each participates in Christ's own salvific death and his resurrection (see Rom 6.5–11). Bound to each other in Christ, each of the baptized, guided by the Spirit, likewise exercises a priestly ministry by acting as Christ's instrument for the salvation of others. The baptized also share in Christ's role as *king.* Subject to Christ's kingship, they are directed to the fullness of his kingdom as their eschatological goal. The loving adoption that is received in baptism urges the faithful to have care for the eternal and present welfare of everyone they encounter (2 Cor 5.14ff). Thus, the baptismal vocation of all those reborn in water and the Spirit demands that they exercise the *tria munera Christi*; that they expect to be ministered to by other Christians who also participate in the threefold office of Christ; and that they give thanks for the gifts deriving from nothing else than the infinitely loving initiative of God. But this participation is no individualistic or purely local matter, for Christians do not belong to Christ without having a relationship with others who likewise

---

[8] See *S&C* §12; see also *Gift* §§11–13; *TCTCV* §19; and *LG* §31. The threefold office of Christ is found in Patristic teaching (Eusebius of Caesarea, John Chrysostom), in the Scholastics (Aquinas), and in Calvin's *Institutes* (II.xv). It was developed in classical Anglicanism by John Pearson in his highly influential *Exposition of the Creed* (1659), significantly referencing Augustine (on Psalm 26) on Christ's body, head, and members. Newman wrote of the Church's participation in the threefold office of Christ in his Preface to the third edition of *The Via Media of the Anglican Church* (1877). See also Paul Avis, *Beyond the Reformation: Authority, Primacy and Unity in the Conciliar Tradition*, pp. 5–12. For further, see §§81 and 83 below.

belong to Christ because the Spirit has given to each a birth to new life in Christ (see *TCTCV* §41).

Belonging to the Church brings a sense of common identity

53. This sense of belonging and 'being claimed' by Christ *in* his body, the Church, carries with it a sense of common identity, calling, and mutual responsibility.[9] Both Anglicans and Catholics can agree that anointed as they are by the Holy One (see 1 Jn 2.20, 27) this body of the faithful, as a whole, will not ultimately depart from the truth on matters necessary to salvation (*LG* §12; *Auth II* §23). No local church has this guarantee in isolation.[10] This indefectibility does not preclude any local church from falling into error for a time. The implication is that indefectibility in teaching demands structures which make this interdependence of the local and trans-local churches and ecclesial bodies function for the growth in truth of the whole Church.

The instinct for the faith of the whole People of God

54. Anglicans and Catholics also recognize that the faithful People of God, thanks to their baptism, share an instinct for the faith (*sensus fidei fidelium*), the spiritual gift of discernment of the truth (see *Gift* §§29–30; also *SFLC*). The sense of faith grows through a life of strong charity and regular religious practice, each of which promotes communion between the faithful and God, who is love. One who loves Love and welcomes Love has a symbiotic relationship with God and, thereby, a sense of who God is, what God expects of us, and the kind of happiness Christ promises. Therefore, the sense of the faith means that the authentic transmission of the faith is not only the preserve of the magisterium and theologians, but also of saintly parents and holy men, women and children who know God 'from within' and have a sense of what conforms to God's designs for human beatitude. The further implication, then, is that

---

9   See WCC Assembly, *Called to Be the One Church*, §7; also Toronto Anglican Congress, 'Mutual Responsibility and Interdependence in the Body of Christ' (1963); *CaC* §43; *Gift* §13.

10   This is also true for the Church of Rome. See, for example, the condemnation of Pope Honorius I by the Third Council of Constantinople (680–1) for asserting the principle of a single will in Christ (Henricus Denzinger, *Enchiridion symbolorum: definitionum et declarationum de rebus fidei et morum*, 36th edn, ed. Adolfus Schönmetzer, Freiburg: Herder, 1976, §552), and the acceptance of that condemnation by Pope Leo II in 683 (Denzinger, *Enchiridion symbolorum*, §563). This is found in Anglican formularies, in particular Article XIX, and in 'classical' Anglican teaching: see, e.g., John Pearson's *Exposition of the Creed* (1659; ed. E. Burton, Oxford: Clarendon Press, 1864), following Calvin.

the Church's indefectibility, as well as the experience of disagreement in the Church, demands structures which will facilitate the fullest possible sharing of the experience of Christ and of the gifts of the Spirit among all the baptized. Through prayer, debate, discussion, and study, the Church at every level seeks consensus with the assistance of the Spirit, even if variously formulated. This process of discernment of the mind of Christ can take time. It is this task of discovering which 'calls for continuing discernment, constant repentance and renewing of the mind (Romans 12)' (*LiC* §29).

The catholicity of the Church

55. The Gospel which proclaims the limitless love and salvific will of God (1 Tim 2.3–4; Jn 3.16) and which is responded to and received in baptism is both deeply personal and local in appropriation and yet necessarily universal in scope and intention (see *Gift* §§26–27; *CaC* §34). It is for this reason that the Church understands itself to be essentially missionary, sent to the whole world. The Great Commission is to preach the Good News from Jerusalem 'to the ends of the earth' (Mt 28.19–20; Acts 1.8) in ways which are intelligible to those who hear it so that they can embrace it with love and fidelity. This means that the Church cannot, without contradiction, become a static self-referential community, nor even a federation of such communities. There is a catholic dimension to the life of the Church at all levels.

The need for instruments of catholicity serving unity and legitimate diversity

56. To *belong* to the Church is thus to belong to a particular, local community that is not turned-in on itself, but reaches beyond itself so that it may truly become a community in full communion with the other communities which form the ecclesial body of Christ and serve the mission of God (see *CaC* §39). For all the rich diversity among the local churches, 'There is one body and one Spirit, just as you were called to the one hope of your calling, one Lord, one faith, one baptism' (Eph 4.4–5). No one can say of any other part of the body, 'I have no need of you' (1 Cor 12.21). Each Christian belongs to a local church and thus shares in the life of every other local church with which that local church is in communion. Since there are thousands of local churches, and a myriad of ways in which the Gospel can be preached, both traditions recognize the need,

variously implemented, for structures of catholicity: instruments of communion serving unity and legitimate diversity. Such respective instruments of communion (see Sections IV–VI) seek to maintain unity in the faith, while supporting the witness and mission of the many churches.

The task of respective instruments of communion

57. Since the faith is received by peoples of different times and cultures, inculturation of the faith means that it will be expressed differently in diverse regions and epochs (see *AL* §3). It is the task of the instruments of communion to ensure both that the faith is handed on intact, and that diversity is maintained where different formulations do not run counter to the faith that is common to all the churches. Instruments of communion also engage with new situations that call sometimes for definitive decisions and at other times for interim decisions (see §148). The task of instruments of communion is to serve the unity and the diversity—the catholicity—of the Church.

The eucharist constitutes and builds up the communion of the Church

The whole Christ is present throughout the action of the eucharist

58. Anglicans and Catholics hold that the communion entered into in baptism reaches its sacramental fullness in the celebration of the eucharist. We believe that 'in the whole action of the eucharist … the crucified and risen Lord, according to his promise offers himself to his people' (*ED* §3). The entire celebration of the eucharist makes 'sacramentally present the whole mystery of salvation' (*ED* §7). Here, through the power of the Spirit, Christ instructs us with his Word and feeds us with his very self. For both traditions, to participate in the eucharist is to be nourished by and taken more deeply into Christ's own life: 'Its purpose is to transmit the life of the crucified and risen Christ to his body, the Church, so that its members may be more fully united with Christ and with one another' (*ED* §6).[11] Reconciled in the eucharist, the faithful are called to be

---

[11] See also 'Our sharing in the body and blood of Christ leads to no other end than that of transforming us into that which we receive.' St Leo the Great, *Sermon 63*, 7, PL 54, 357; and 'The life-giving Word of God by uniting himself with his own flesh made it also life-giving. And so it was right that he should be united with our bodies through his sacred flesh and precious blood, which we receive as a life-giving blessing in the bread and wine.' St Cyril of Alexandria, Commentary on Lk 22.19, PG 72, 92.

servants of reconciliation, justice, and peace, and witnesses to the joy of the resurrection.[12]

In the eucharist the Church both meets Christ and is there disclosed to itself

59.　As in baptism, eucharistic participation in Christ is not merely individualistic but is necessarily collective and ecclesial: 'The cup of blessing that we bless, is it not a sharing [*koinonia*] in the blood of Christ? The bread that we break, is it not a sharing [*koinonia*] in the body of Christ? Because there is one bread, we who are many are one body, for we all partake of the one bread' (1 Cor 10.16–17). The eucharist celebrates and affirms the traditional understanding of the identity of the entire Church as born from the blood (signifying the eucharist) and water (signifying baptism) that flowed from the side of the crucified Christ (Jn 19.34). Furthermore, the risen and ascended Christ, present in the eucharist, always resides within the Church which is his Spirit-filled, charism-endowed body (1 Cor 12–14). In the eucharist, the Church both meets Christ and is there disclosed to itself. St Augustine famously gave eloquent expression to this in the context of exploring with the newly baptized what it means to receive communion:

> *If you are the body and members of Christ, it is your mystery which is placed on the Lord's table; it is your mystery you receive. It is to that which you are that you answer 'Amen', and by that response you make your assent. You hear the words 'the body of Christ'; you answer 'Amen'. Be a member of Christ, so that the 'Amen' may be true. ... Be what you see; receive what you are. (Sermon 272)*

The eucharist both celebrates communion and deepens the desire for communion

60.　Authentic eucharistic participation in Christ is, then, always an ecclesial participation. Eucharistic communion with Christ is communion with all who similarly share in Christ through the Spirit (*Gift* §13; see also *LG* §7). The eucharist nourishes and feeds this ecclesial body of Christ and impels those who share in it towards the

---

[12] See 1 Cor 11.17–34, particularly 22 and 29; also Mt 25.31–46; Gal 2.10; 1 Cor 16.1–4; 2 Cor 8.1–15, 9.6–15. For St John Chrysostom's development of this theme, see 'The Gospel of St Matthew: Homily L.4', PG 58, 508–9.

overcoming of all that obstructs or weakens this communion.[13] For this reason, as is often noted in ecumenical contexts, the eucharist both celebrates the communion that already exists and intensifies in us the desire to move to deeper communion, for 'has Christ been divided?' (1 Cor 1.13). In celebrating and living the eucharist the Church becomes more fully what it is. St Augustine describes the eucharist as the sacrament 'through which in the present age the Church is made' (*Contra Faustum*, 12, 20). The eucharist is the living memorial of Christ's sacrificial death in which the Church entreats the benefits of his passion and enters into the movement of his self-offering (see *ED* §5).

The eucharist celebrated in communion with the bishop actualizes the fullness of ecclesial reality

61. Within each of our traditions the fullness of ecclesial reality, situated within the communion of the Trinity, is understood to be actualized when a specific community celebrates the eucharist in full communion with its bishop, thereby sharing in the eternal liturgy of heaven and in the communion of all the churches (see *LG* §26). In this regard, St Ignatius of Antioch articulated the principle that 'Where the bishop is, there is the church' (*Letter to theP Smyrnaeans,* ch. 8). In neither tradition, then, is the local church regarded as but an incomplete part of a greater whole. 'Each local church contains within it the fullness of what it is to be the Church. It is wholly Church, but not the whole Church' (*TCTCV* §31).[14] However, this ecclesial fullness in the local church does not, for either tradition, imply an isolated, independent self-sufficiency.

Ecclesial communion: local and trans-local

The Church as communion: what we share and how we differ

62. The shared ecclesiology outlined in the previous section is much indebted to *The Final Report* (1982), *Church as Communion* (1991), and *The Gift of Authority* (1999). It highlights our shared understanding of the relation, within communion, of the local, trans-local,

---

[13] See *LG* §11; also *LG* §3. Contemporary Anglican eucharistic piety and liturgy celebrate the same conviction in the adaptation of St Paul's plea for the unity of the Corinthian Church: 'Though we are many, we are one body, because we all share in one bread.'

[14] See also *LG* §23; also General Synod of the Church of England, 'The Governance of the Church of England and the Anglican Communion' (7 January 2009), GS Misc 910, §2.2.

and universal levels of the Church. Each of the above-mentioned Agreed Statements demonstrates a significant area of agreement between our two traditions. There are, however, also significant differences, and it is in this area that we believe ecclesial repentance and receptive learning can take place.

Worldwide communion for Catholics is determined by communion with the Bishop of Rome

63. For the Catholic Church, it is possible for one local church to be in communion with another local church only when the bishop of each is in communion with the Bishop of Rome (see *LG* §23 and *CN* §13). One local Catholic church cannot be in full communion with another local church whose bishop is not in communion with the Bishop of Rome.

Worldwide communion for Anglicans with the Archbishop of Canterbury

64. Anglicans hold an understanding of a global communion centred on the See of Canterbury. The consequences for Anglicans of communion with the Archbishop of Canterbury differ from the consequences for Catholics of communion with the Bishop of Rome. Currently within the Anglican Communion there exist provincial churches which are in communion with the Archbishop of Canterbury but refuse to be in communion with other provincial churches that are also in communion with the Archbishop of Canterbury (see LC 1998, Resolution IV.11). There are also provincial churches in communion with the Archbishop of Canterbury which claim communion with other churches that are not in communion with the Archbishop of Canterbury. For Anglicans all of these situations are anomalous, and some are deeply painful. Other anomalies, of a more positive kind, are found, for example, in the full communion relationships shared between Lutherans and Anglicans in both the USA and Canada. Lambeth 1998 stated that '... some anomalies may be bearable when there is an agreed goal of visible unity, but ... there should always be an impetus towards their resolution and, thus, towards the removal of the principal anomaly of disunity' (Resolution IV.1.3).

Differences in levels of decisions about ecumenical recognition

65. As the previous paragraphs suggest, decisions about the recognition of communion with other churches are taken at different levels

in Anglican and Catholic structures. Anglican provinces can individually and regionally decide to enter into ecumenical agreements entailing the sharing of communion or the mutual recognition of ministries without this decision necessarily having any direct implications for other churches of the Anglican Communion.[15] For Catholics, such decisions could only be taken at the universal level, so that they would have direct implications for all Roman Catholic churches and Eastern Catholic churches throughout the world.

Differences in levels of decision-making demonstrate differences of understanding

66. This difference between our two traditions goes to the heart of a difference of understanding and structure between the Roman Catholic Church and the churches of the Anglican Communion. In the Roman Catholic tradition, policy decisions about communion are made at the universal level; in the Anglican tradition, at the national or provincial level. In part this relates to different understandings as to how the Church moves forward in unity, mission, and truth. At issue is the balance between responsiveness to the demands of specific contexts and the need to move together. This reflects the inheritance of the juridical split in the sixteenth century between the Church of England, with its national (trans-local) identity, and the Church of Rome, with its universal horizon.

For Catholics: the question of the priority of the universal or local church

67. For Catholics a further key question concerns the ecclesial reality of the universal Church, symbolized and structured in terms of the primacy of the See of Rome. Does the universal Church have temporal and ontological priority over the local churches and regional bodies, with the latter being derived from and dependent upon the prior reality of the universal? Or should the universal and the local be viewed as mutually defining, coexistent, and necessarily co-inhering, so that the universal Church has

---

[15] e.g. the British and Irish Anglican Churches with the Nordic and Baltic Lutheran Churches in the Porvoo Agreement; also the agreement between The Episcopal Church and the Evangelical Lutheran Church in America and between the Evangelical Lutheran Church in Canada and the Anglican Church of Canada.

responsibilities towards the local churches, and the local churches have responsibilities both towards one another and towards the universal Church?[16]

What is at issue for Catholics

68. The first of these options reflects the concern that the universal Church should not be viewed as a merely secondary federal reality that derives from the cooperation of the local churches (*CN* §§8–9). It is important to note that this concern can be adequately accommodated while also allowing that the multiplicity of the local churches is constitutive of the universal through what has been called a 'special relationship of "mutual interiority"' (*CN* §9). This multiplicity does not, in its diversity, need to be viewed as a derived and subordinate secondary reality.

Differences in practice over episcopal appointments

69. These questions and tensions have bearing on practical matters in the life of our traditions, such as the procedures for episcopal appointments (see §§91–92), concerning which there has been considerable historical variation.

Differences within the Anglican Communion over provincial autonomy: the proposed Covenant

70. The process of debate about the proposed Anglican Communion Covenant demonstrates that there are considerable differences of perspective and judgement within the Anglican Communion as to what is implied by being in ecclesial communion and what should be the appropriate balance between trans-local autonomy and mutual accountability. The debate has centred on whether there is any place or need within the Anglican Communion for central structures of decision-making and authority on matters that pertain to all. The distinctive histories and understandings of the various provinces of the Communion have meant that, thus far at least, its identity has been characterized by a very high degree of provincial autonomy.

---

[16] See *LG* §23. See also Anglican–Roman Catholic Consultation in the United States, *Agreed Report on the Local/Universal Church* (15 November 1999).

The need for effective structures and instruments of communion in service of mission and unity

71. *Church as Communion* demonstrates the extent to which Catholics and Anglicans share a common understanding of communion ecclesiology. This concept of communion is an invisible union of the baptized with the divine Trinity and with one another, and a reality that demands visible expression served by a common life of liturgy, doctrine, and institutional structures (see *CaC* §15 and *CN* §§3–4). In the life of the Church this communion is articulated in teaching, practice, policy, procedure, and structure. In neither tradition is it acceptable for the understanding of Church to remain at the level of the gathered congregation, either in the parish or in the diocese. For Anglicans there are strong bonds of affection between diverse local and provincial/regional churches that imply recognition and regard for each other. However, within these bonds of affection Anglicans are seeking more robust forms of mutual accountability. Anglicans and Catholics recognize the need for instruments of communion that serve the sustaining and furtherance of such communion (*CaC* §45). The question remains to what extent these instruments of communion need to be both *affective* (i.e. focused on transmitting a loving spirit of communion and ecclesial cooperation) and *effective* (i.e. implying practices of mutual accountability, shared governance, and decision-making).

Instruments of communion: willed by the Lord but reformable in function

72. Furthermore, given the Lord's will that his followers remain united in their love for one another (Jn 13.34–35; 17.21ff), the gift of such ministerial instruments of communion can be held to be willed by the Lord (see Jn 21.15–17; Acts 20.28ff; Eph 4.11–13). Our common reading of the New Testament and post-apostolic period leads Catholics and Anglicans to agree that *episcope*, synodality, and primacy are enduring and necessary, and are gifts of God for the unity and mission of the Church (see §§33–35 and 41–44). Roman Catholic teaching holds that episcopacy, including collegiality, and primacy are essential to the Church. It is important, however, also to note that the specific manner of their structure and functioning can, and has, assumed very different forms and therefore can be renewed and reformed. The

exercise of these instruments has often been the subject of controversy and debate.

Instruments of communion in the Anglican Communion

73. In this regard the churches of the Anglican Communion have developed the following instruments of communion, aimed at promoting mutual accountability among the provinces and national churches at the global level: the Archbishop of Canterbury, the Lambeth Conference, the Anglican Consultative Council, and the Primates' Meeting. Meanwhile *within* the provinces and national churches, variously determined according to specific historical and contextual factors, are provincial and national synods with respective houses of bishops, clergy, and laity. These synods are decision-making bodies which share in the responsibility for unity, faith, and order inherent in the episcopal office. Similarly, within the dioceses the same three-tiered synodal processes operate. Diocesan synods are, in some parts of the Anglican Communion, supported by deanery synods and, at the parish level, by parochial pastoral councils in which clergy and laity debate and decide issues together.

Instruments of communion in the Roman Catholic Church

74. The Roman Catholic Church, affirming the divine institution of the college of bishops and its head, the Bishop of Rome, has developed instruments of communion at the level of the universal Church: (i) the regular and extraordinary meetings of the Synod of Bishops convened by the Bishop of Rome as head of the college (*CIC* c. 344) and also in the potential exceptional convening of a full council of the college of bishops (*CIC* c. 338); (ii) the Roman Curia. The college of cardinals also serves the primacy by electing the Bishop of Rome. At the intermediate level of inter-diocesan, intra-regional communion there are: national and regional bishops' conferences and their associated offices and committees; the regular *ad limina* collective visits of the bishops of a particular region or of a national bishops' conference to Rome (*CIC* cc. 399–400); and canonical provision for the possibility of regional/national synods, involving bishops, priests, deacons, religious, and laity. At the level of the diocesan church and parish congregations, canonically required instruments of communion include: diocesan episcopal councils, councils of diocesan clergy, and diocesan and parochial finance

committees. In addition, Latin rite canon law allows for, but does not require, diocesan pastoral councils, diocesan synods, and parish and deanery councils.

Problems with instruments of communion both within and between churches

75. While Anglicans and Catholics variously recognize the need for instruments of communion, these differing offices, structures, and procedures present problems not only in the inter-ecclesial context—concerning relations between the traditions and mutual recognition across significant differences—but also *within* respective Anglican and Roman Catholic intra-ecclesial life. In each tradition there is ongoing debate as to how adequate these instruments of communion are to serve the current needs of mission and unity. Each tradition experiences its own particular tensions within the ecclesial body of Christ.

The Roman Catholic concern over the ministry of the Bishop of Rome

76. In the Roman Catholic context, there are signs of an openness to reconsidering the role of the papacy. This was brought to prophetic focus by Pope John Paul II in his 1995 encyclical *Ut Unum Sint*. When acknowledging Christ's desire for the unity of all Christian communities, he spoke of finding a way to 'exercise primacy' without 'renouncing what is essential to its mission', while being open 'to a new situation'. He invited leaders and theologians of other churches to engage with him in 'a patient and fraternal' dialogue about how the particular ministry of unity of the Bishop of Rome might be exercised in new circumstances (*UUS* §§95–96; *Gift* §4). Pope Francis in *Evangelii Gaudium* reiterates this call with urgency (§32).

Anglican concern over the adequacy and limits of the existing instruments at the various levels of ecclesial life

77. The Lambeth Conference emerged in the nineteenth century in the context of concerns facing an emerging global communion of churches. In the early twentieth century, tensions arose over moral issues (e.g. polygamy, artificial contraception, the remarriage of divorced persons) and from the mid-twentieth century, the ordination of women to the presbyterate and episcopate. From

the late twentieth century into the twenty-first century, the most acute tensions have concerned questions of human sexuality. These issues also arise in Roman Catholic contexts. In Anglican contexts, however, they represent a new situation because of the apparent inability of the instruments of communion at the worldwide level both to resolve the presenting issues themselves and to find agreed-upon processes – such as those in the proposed Anglican Communion Covenant (see §137 and n. 48) – to contain conflict so that it does not lead to further impairment of communion. This new situation raises questions about the adequacy and limits of the existing instruments at the various levels of Anglican ecclesial life. Indeed, it highlights the tension between the inheritance of doctrine that Anglicans share (rooted in the interpretation of Scripture and the interpretation of moral norms) and its different expressions in local and regional contexts.[17]

The need in this situation for mutual receptive learning

78.   Today's sober appreciation of the long-term nature of the ecumenical calling (see §§5–6 and 10) has coincided with the recognition *within* each of our traditions of our respective difficulties and the need for processes of reform and renewal. We suggest that the current twofold task, as we seek to walk the way towards full communion, is (i) to look humbly at what is not working effectively *within one's own tradition*, and (ii) to ask whether this might be helped by receptive learning from the understanding, structures, practices, and judgements of the other. The opportunity is to teach by showing what it means to learn and to bear witness by showing what it means to receive in our need—recognizing that at times the members of one tradition may judge that the practices and structures of the other will not, in a given instance, be helpful.

---

[17] e.g. in response to the question of blessing same-sex relationships, the 'St Michael Report' of the Anglican Church of Canada explores the dynamic tension between core doctrine and other doctrines: '[A] distinction is recognized between what may be termed "core doctrines" and what may be termed *adiaphora* … Core doctrines have been understood … to mean the credal and earliest conciliar explications of Scripture with regard to the doctrine of the Trinity and the person and work of Jesus Christ. *Adiaphora* have been defined as matters "upon which disagreement can be tolerated without endangering unity" (*WR* §A.36).' The Anglican Church of Canada, 'The St Michael Report' (May 2005), §8. See also the IARCCUM sub-committee report 'Ecclesiological Reflections on the Current Situation in the Anglican Communion in the Light of ARCIC', *Information Service*, 119/3 (2005), 102–11.

The structure of the next three sections

79. The following sections of this document explore the effectiveness of the respective instruments of communion within the Anglican Communion and the Roman Catholic Church at the three levels of diocesan churches and parochial eucharistic communities (Section IV); regional churches and structures (Section V); and worldwide communion / universal Church (Section VI). In each case, the first concern is to map what currently pertains in the traditions, the second to identify and analyse where the points of systemic tension are, and the third to ask where, relative to what is weak, or less developed, in one tradition, there may be fruitful learning from what is strong in the other. This is to build explicitly on previous phases of ARCIC dialogue and to take them forward in a spirit of receptive ecumenical learning so that both separately and jointly our traditions can continue to walk the way of conversion and witness to the communion of God in Christ and the Spirit. It is in this way that this document serves the mandate of the Commission to explore how the traditions respectively understand and practise the interrelationship of the various levels of the Church in discernment and decision-making (see §§10–13).

IV. Instruments of Communion at the Local Levels of Anglican and Roman Catholic Life

As explained in the Co-Chairs' Preface and in §79, this section has three main subsections: IV.A describes what currently is the case for each of our traditions concerning the respective instruments of communion which operate at this level; IV.B identifies what respective tensions and difficulties are experienced in relation to these instruments of communion at this level; IV.C asks what possibilities there might be for transformative receptive learning from the other tradition in relation to these tensions and difficulties. The Commission has chosen to present our structures, our challenges, and our learnings in parallel columns. At times, in order to avoid appearing to equate quite different processes, we use a sequential format, but with those paragraphs on the left-hand side of the page in an Anglican voice, and those on the right-hand side in a Roman Catholic voice.

80. Anglicans and Catholics each recognize the need for effective instruments of communion to sustain and further ecclesial communion at the various levels of church life (§§71–73; *CaC* §45). Each tradition also experiences systemic stress in relation to these instruments of communion and so recognizes the need to reform or reconfigure them (§§75–77). We now turn to examine these instruments in some detail. There is a need in our ecumenical dialogues to talk about the lived reality of the structures that sustain the churches—their strengths and their weaknesses. We begin with the reality of the Church as it is most widely experienced, therefore, the parish, and beyond that the diocese, examining how they are structured and governed and why so. Sometimes the forces of theology, culture, and circumstance have seen us diverge, and at other times, more happily, we have discovered the bond of a common experience and jointly held principles. However, to speak of our reality, we must also speak of our woundedness, recognizing ourselves as disciples who repeatedly fail in our attempts to live the Gospel call of Christ. Acknowledging our weakness, in the company of our Christian brothers and sisters, opens us to the possibility of learning from them and receiving healing.

IV.A Instruments of communion at the local levels of Anglican and Roman Catholic life

Shared understanding of the *tria munera Christi*

81. Traditionally Christ's threefold messianic activity as prophet, priest, and king (see Heb 7–10) has been identified as a gift that is shared with the Church. All the baptized participate in Christ's *tria munera* of teaching, sanctifying, and leading God's people (see also §§52, 83). The baptized are empowered by the Holy Spirit to share the Gospel in word and action; they are formed and nurtured in eucharistic communities; and they share with the ordained in discerning and serving the needs of mission, ministry, and management. The bishop delegates responsibility to presbyters, deacons, and authorized lay ministers for the liturgical, sacramental, and pastoral life of congregations. Because lay people participate in the threefold gifts of Christ they have a shared responsibility with the presbyter for matters of parochial life.

Shared structures of parish, bishop, and diocese

82. For most Anglicans and Catholics, the parish is the normal locus of Christian formation. There the Word of God is solemnly proclaimed, and the eucharist and the other sacraments of Christian initiation celebrated. The parishes are held in unity under the guidance and authority of a bishop who is the visible sign of communion with all the wider levels of the Church. The bishop is the key instrument of communion for the local church. In this the bishop works with consultative or deliberative structures and procedures involving clergy and laity. In Roman Catholic structures such participation is generally consultative.

Complementary sharing in the threefold offices and authority of Christ

83. In Anglican polity and practice, authority is dispersed among and between laity, deacons, *Lumen Gentium* recognizes that each of the baptized share in Christ's *tria munera*.[18] The

---

[18] See §81. Although there was a Patristic tradition affirming that the baptized Christian had been anointed prophet, priest, and king, medieval theology made little reference to the threefold office except when describing the ministry of the ordained. Official Catholic teaching continued to reserve express application of the *tria munera* to the ordained until the Second Vatican Council, where, through the influence of John Henry Newman and Yves Congar, it extended the motif to the laity and the sanctifying, teaching, and governing functions of Christ's ministry to the role of the Church as *a whole*.

presbyters, and bishops in a manner believed to be a manifestation of the Holy Spirit's guidance of the community. This presumes the necessary and adequate spiritual formation of each for discernment.

Anglicans understand both that all the baptized partake in Christ's mission of teaching, sanctifying, and governing (*tria munera*) and that the episcopate has a particular role therein. Anglican canons, constitutions, and liturgies reflect the distinct ways in which laity, clergy, and bishops share in this mission.

Typically, priest and parish jointly appoint and elect lay churchwardens (an ancient office predating the Reformation) to oversee the temporal responsibilities of parochial life (e.g. building maintenance, financial management). A further group of laity is elected and/or appointed as a parish council (presided over by the parish priest or duly appointed lay person) for regular consultation and shared decision-making between annual meetings. Other non-parochial appointments and ministries also involve

participation of the baptized in Christ's priesthood and the participation of the ordained in that same priesthood are 'directed toward each other' as distinct exercises of the one priesthood of Christ (*LG* §10).

There has been a tendency in Roman Catholic theology to distinguish between the participation of the ordained in the *tria munera* as primarily ordered internally towards the Christian community, and that of the laity as primarily externally directed towards the world.[19] While this distinction still holds, laity are now involved in both arenas.

Since the Second Vatican Council, in most places, there has been a burgeoning of lay participation in the Roman Catholic Church at nearly every level and in nearly every kind of ministry in which the Church is involved (*CFL* §2). The laity are not only widely involved in the temporal affairs of the Church (such as finance councils) but have become the primary educators of the faithful in preparation for reception of the sacraments and have been consulted widely through diocesan

---

[19] e.g. *LG* §10 describes the ministerial priest as one who, 'by the sacred power he enjoys, teaches and rules the priestly people'. At §31 the same document states: 'What specifically characterises the laity is their secular nature', and envisages the exercise of their common priesthood 'by engaging in temporal affairs and by ordering them according to the plan of God' and thereby working 'for the sanctification of the world from within as a leaven'; see also *AA* §2; and *CFL* §15.

structures which are ultimately accountable to the diocesan bishop.

In addition to the structural involvement of the laity, it is normal for laity to exercise pastoral and teaching roles, including that of lay theologian and the offices of catechist and reader. Lay persons assist in the distribution of Holy Communion as eucharistic ministers. Lay persons are regularly appointed as diocesan chancellors.

synods that advise bishops on a broad variety of issues. In some parts of the world laity are appointed as chancellors of dioceses and lead diocesan offices. Seminaries now employ lay faculty members. Laity can also function as catechists, educators, lay theologians, extraordinary ministers of holy communion, and pastoral ministers. All such participation of the laity is at the discretion of clergy and bishops.

Similarly, those bodies which are composed of laity and which deal with matters of Church polity, such as parish councils and diocesan synods, are called at the discretion of the parish priest or bishop. The involvement of laity in them is of a consultative nature.

Deacons and presbyters as co-workers of the bishop

84. In accord with ancient tradition, Anglicans and Catholics view deacons and presbyters as sharing in the bishop's ministry in the Church (*MO* §9). The Second Vatican Council's *Presbyterorum Ordinis* speaks of the 'office of priests' as sharing 'in its own degree' in the *tria munera* of Christ in order to be co-workers with the bishop in teaching, sanctifying, and governing the diocese (*PO* §2). Similarly, *Lumen Gentium* speaks of deacons as 'also sharers in the mission and grace of the Supreme Priest' (§41) and thereby assisting in the pastoral care of the diocese. In Anglican ordinals, deacons are called to work with the bishop, sharing in the pastoral ministry of the Church. Presbyters are similarly charged to work with their bishop and fellow ministers (e.g. the Ordinal of the Church of England in *Common Worship*).

85. For Anglicans and Catholics alike, in all cases the appointment and authorization to preach and administer the sacraments are granted

by the diocesan bishop or other ordinary. The licensing of clergy in Anglican polity mirrors the granting of faculties in Roman Catholic terms.

86. There is a range of ways in which Anglican clergy are appointed to parishes and other ministries by the bishop. The process of appointment may include consultation with laity in the nomination of candidates, advertisement of vacancies, or direct episcopal appointment.

Latin rite canon law stipulates that 'appointment to the office of parish priest belongs to the diocesan bishop, who is free to confer it on whomsoever he pleases' (*CIC* c. 523). Involvement of the laity in the selection process is undertaken at the discretion of the bishop.

The role of bishops

87. Anglicans and Catholics largely share an understanding of the role of the bishop that stems from the ancient common tradition of the Church. Endowed by episcopal ordination with a special 'sacramental charism' for the office, the bishop is regarded as the primary minister of Word and sacrament and leader in the exercise of the *tria munera* of Christ to teach, sanctify, and rule in the diocese.[20]

88. Bishops play a crucial part in maintaining the unity of the Church catholic. They are the successors to the apostles in that individually they have oversight over the Church of God and its mission in a particular place and corporately they ensure that the Church is maintained in truth. Bishops are to teach the faith and ensure sound preaching and the provision of the sacraments. When the diocesan church assembles for the eucharist, it is the bishop who presides, supported by the presbyters and deacons, with the full participation of God's holy people.[21] It is the bishop's duty to ensure, through the selection and ordination of deacons and presbyters, that the parishes remain flourishing eucharistic communities which care actively for the poor and excluded.

---

[20] See *PCL* §37.3; also *LG* §21; *CIC* c. 375; Appendix II, 'The Anglican Way', in *Communion, Conflict and Hope: The Kuala Lumpur Report of the Third Inter-Anglican Theological and Doctrinal Commission* (London: Anglican Communion Office, 2008), pp. 57–8.

[21] See *PCL* §31.5: 'A bishop has oversight to govern, teach and minister, a priest shares with and assists the bishop in the care of souls, and a deacon assists these; all are called to fulfil a ministry appropriate to their particular order.' See also *SC* §41.

89. The bishop is concerned not only for the faithfulness of the local church, but also for the faithfulness of all the other local churches.[22] Bishops are to support one another in their ministry, acting together as guardians of the faith. They listen to the clergy and laity of their own diocese and represent the experience and insights of their diocese more widely within the Church. They listen to the experience and insights of the wider Church and represent them to their own diocese. In this way, bishops serve to communicate 'what the Spirit is saying to the churches' (Rev 2.7, 11, 17, 29; 3.6, 13, 22) and help the churches respond in penitence and faith. It is because the bishop always acts in communion that both the Catholic Church and the Anglican Communion follow the practice of the Church since at least the fourth century of normally having at least three bishops participate in the ordination of a new bishop (see Council of Nicaea 325, Canon 4).

The authority of the bishop as an instrument of communion

90. A key feature of Anglican episcopacy is the 'bishop-in-synod', at both diocesan and provincial levels. In Anglican polity the diocesan bishop presides in consultation with the clergy and laity of the diocese. The consent of the diocesan bishop is required for any resolution of a diocesan synod to be enacted. This protects the role of the bishop as 'guardian of the faith and unity of the church'. This pattern of the 'bishop-in-synod' is mirrored across the Communion.

Sacramental ordination and hierarchical communion with the Bishop of Rome give the diocesan ordinaries 'all the ordinary, proper and immediate power which is required for the exercise of their pastoral office', without prejudice to prerogatives of the Supreme Pontiff (*CD* §8).

The Second Vatican Council envisaged that, in the governance of the diocese, the bishop would be assisted by various individuals and advisory bodies

---

[22] The model homily for the Roman Catholic Ordination Rite for Bishops instructs the new bishop, 'Never forget that in the Catholic Church, made one by the bond of Christian love, you are incorporated into the college of bishops. *You should therefore have a constant concern for all the churches* (own italics) and gladly come to the aid and support of churches in need.' *Roman Pontifical*, Rite of Ordination of a Bishop 39, Homily; see also *CD* §5 and *AS* §2. Similarly, a teaching document of the Church of England House of Bishops speaks of the collegial ministry of bishops as belonging 'within a connectedness of gracious belonging, operating at the local, national and international spheres of the life of the Church' and as maintaining 'the local church/diocese in fellowship—in communion—with the Church around the world'. Church of England, *Bishops in Communion: Collegiality in Service of the Koinonia of the Church*, p. 38.

(*CD* §27). Latin rite canon law makes provision, at the discretion of the bishop, for a diocesan synod (c. 461) and a pastoral council, each of which can include laity (c. 463). In addition, it mandates the formation both of a council of priests and a college of consultors. These bodies are consultative since the bishop is 'sole legislator', by whose authority decrees are published (c. 391, §2). In the Eastern Catholic churches, the only obligatory diocesan synodal structure is the presbyteral council and a subgroup of that, the eparchial (diocesan) college. Pastoral councils, which are consultative, may include Christians, either lay or clerical, of other Catholic churches (*CCEO* cc. 264–75).

The selection of bishops

91. The processes for selecting bishops in both the Anglican Communion and the Roman Catholic Church have a common aim: choosing candidates who will preserve the Church in a unity of faith, sacramental practice, and mission to others. Inasmuch as the bishop will not be effective unless the candidate is acceptable to the community and to the college of bishops who together have the responsibility of articulating the faith and shepherding the flock, both of our traditions employ procedures that seek to guarantee the selection of effective candidates. Thus, in both of our communions, the consent of the baptized and the approval of fellow bishops are desired before episcopal ordination occurs. Both of our traditions honour the ancient practices that saw the local church, assisted by the leadership of neighbouring churches, select (*eligere*) its bishop. But each has its particular emphasis.

92. Anglican procedures involve direct participation of the laity, clergy, and bishops. A diocesan bishop is either elected or appointed for ordination (or translation if already in episcopal orders) from among priests with the requisite qualifications as defined by the province in its own canon law. There is a variety of consultative practices around the Anglican Communion. In many jurisdictions the election requires the majority support of the clergy and laity separately. The nomination requires confirmation by the diocesan bishops or regional metropolitan.[23] Bishops who assist a diocesan bishop may be appointed or elected according to the practice of the diocese or province.

Although appointment or approval by the Bishop of Rome is mandatory, Roman Catholic procedures, in different ways, may involve consulting laity, religious, priests, and other bishops.

Latin rite canon law states, 'The Supreme Pontiff freely appoints bishops or confirms those legitimately elected' (c. 377). In much of the world, the Papal Nuncio of a given territory, having consulted local clergy and, often, vowed religious and laity, sends a list of three names (*terna*) to the appropriate Vatican Congregation, which then presents the name and dossier of the candidate it considers most suitable to the Pope.

In some places, cathedral canons either elect a candidate or propose a *terna* for their own diocese. In still others, the canons select someone from a *terna* proposed to them by the Pope.

The Code of Canons of the Eastern Churches (*CCEO*) specifies that the relevant synod of bishops identifies names of potential candidates for the episcopate. In this task it may enlist the help of presbyters and

---

23 In the Church of England, diocesan bishops are appointed by the Crown after nomination by a commission which includes bishops, clergy, and laity both from the diocese and from the appropriate province of the two which constitute the Church of England.

the laity. The names of potential candidates are sent to the Pope for his approval. Later, when the synod elects someone to become a bishop, if the one selected has already been approved, his ordination may take place forthwith. If the one selected has not been previously approved, he must be approved by the Pope before he can be ordained.[24]

IV.B Tensions and difficulties in the practice of communion at the local levels of Anglican and Roman Catholic life

The challenges posed by parochialism and liturgy

93.   Both Anglicans and Catholics are often criticized for a parochialism that undervalues the necessary connection with the wider Church, either from the parish to the diocesan level or from the diocese to the regional and worldwide levels. Similarly, both traditions experience disagreements about that which should be the clearest expression of our respective communion, our worship. While both traditions authorize a number of rites, we each experience tensions and sometimes divisions focused on liturgical practices.

94.

The question of an ethos of collaborative discernment in Anglican synodal structures	*The question of structures and processes for the deliberative involvement of the laity in diocesan and parochial governance*
The cooperation of laity, clergy, and bishops in discernment at the diocesan level is a strength that Anglicans value. The legislative focus of a diocesan synod can, however, eclipse the	The tendency towards an internal/external understanding of clerical distinctiveness (see §83) means that lay participation in ecclesial governance is generally consultative and

---

[24] See *CCEO* cc. 182–5. Here and elsewhere, in terms of numbers the examples drawn from the Eastern Catholic churches represent a minority of cases. However, we cite them because of their ecclesiological significance.

need for catechesis and renewal in this forum. In contexts of sharp division, the oppositional style of parliamentary decision-making, usually required by synodical structures, can sometimes be a blunt instrument with which to decide responses to sensitive pastoral needs and doctrinal and ethical questions. Internal theological differences can sometimes degenerate into partisan attitudes.

non-deliberative, whether in parish councils, diocesan synods, diocesan pastoral councils, or the appointment of bishops and parish priests. Nor are such structures and processes mandatory. Even while recognizing the need to preserve the executive roles of bishops within dioceses and parish priests in parishes, the current models of governance seem not to give adequate recognition to the anointing of all the baptized and their share in the Good Shepherd's pastoral ministry (*AA* §2). The reciprocal dependence on and ordering to each other of the laity and the ordained is not sufficiently expressed. Given that the whole body of the baptized has an unfailing instinct for the faith (see §§53–54), the distinctive teaching role of bishops is to bring this to explicit articulation. The lay faithful, for their part, not only receive teaching, but also offer their own expertise and faith to the Church. Moreover, they bring with their faith their gifts and talents for the service of the Church. These two circumstances, at least, call for even greater lay involvement in teaching and in the management of dioceses and parishes.

95. *Trans-jurisdictional accountability within and across dioceses*

The need for executive accountability to the faithful at diocesan and parochial levels

In recent years internal divisions over issues of gender and human sexuality have sometimes led parishes and clergy within a diocese into open disagreement with their diocesan bishop and synod. Some wish to place themselves under the jurisdiction of a bishop of another diocese from a different province. In an effort to offer a mutually acceptable practice of oversight that is compatible with the theological and juridical authority of a diocesan bishop, models of delegated episcopal oversight have been established in some provinces. It is unclear whether these are to be viewed as enduring features of Anglican polity or as temporary anomalies while the church in question continues its discernment of particular issues. A degree of impaired communion is seen as the cost of a settlement which respects the integrity of conscience.

Sometimes bishops and parish priests have an authority of governance that is without sufficient checks and balances on the part of those governed. By this authority decisions can be taken without involving a process of negotiation with the wider parish or diocesan community. There are no structures in place for allowing the governed to have recourse within the parish or diocese concerning grievances at the respective level. Canon law permits only recourse to higher authority, and higher authority sometimes responds simply on the basis of whether the correct canonical procedures were followed in a case.

96.

The need for Roman Catholic fora for lay discussion, debate, and disagreement

The instinct for unity and participation in the greater whole of the universal Church is a deeply embedded value within the Roman Catholic tradition which is given structural and sacramental form through communion with the Bishop of Rome. This is a defining instinct and core gift of Roman Catholicism. This instinct for unity can, however, result in the suppression of difference, the inhibiting of candid conversation, and the avoidance of contentious issues in open fora. While the Second Vatican Council recognized the participation of all the baptized in the *tria munera*, and while Roman Catholic theology recognizes their role in discerning teaching through the *sensus fidei*, this recognition has not yet fully permeated Roman Catholic habits of mind and discourse. The consultative processes at national and diocesan levels associated with and in the Synods (2014–16) concerning marriage and the family express a positive change in this regard.

Church growth, vocations to the ordained ministry, and current challenges

97. While from 1970 to 2015 the overall population of the Anglican Communion grew from 47 to 86 million people,[25] there have been parts of the Anglican Communion—Europe, North In most countries, even in countries with an absolute increase in the number of presbyters, there is an insufficiency of priests seen in an increase in the ratio of Catholics to priest.[26] Worldwide,

---

[25] The most current survey of Anglican statistical information is from David Goodhew (ed.), *Growth and Decline in the Anglican Communion, 1980 to the Present.*

[26] Center for Applied Research in the Apostolate, at: http://cara.georgetown.edu/frequently-requested-church-statistics; see also *Annuarium Statisticum Ecclesiae 2015* (Vatican City, 2017).

America, Australia—that have experienced significant decline. Both growth and decline have posed serious new challenges to the inherited pattern of full-time stipendiary parish-based clergy, including the cost of maintaining full-time paid clergy and their families. New developments from the inherited pattern have emerged throughout the Anglican Communion in recent decades, such as the rise of non-stipendiary clergy, alternative models of theological and pastoral formation, locally discerned clergy, and the grouping of diverse local congregations into a larger geographical parish served by a single priest or team ministry. While the ordination of women did not arise as a response to the increased demand for ministry caused by Church growth, the growing numbers of female deacons, priests, and bishops have played a very significant role in meeting the pastoral needs of new congregations. Lastly, throughout the Anglican Communion, the fruits of ecumenical dialogue at the provincial levels have also seen the emergence of ecumenically 'shared ministries' or local ecumenical projects.

the number of Catholics per parish has increased from 3,759 in 1980 to 5,759 in 2015. In some countries, this lack of priests has led to the closure of parishes; in others, the number of parishes and clergy has not kept up with the increasing number of faithful. As well as praying for and seeking to nurture vocations within existing models, many Catholics are being led by this situation to ask whether worshipping communities need new forms or models of ministry in order to continue or thrive.

IV.C Potential receptive ecclesial learning at the local levels of Anglican and Roman Catholic life

98. *Anglican receptive learning about the possibility of parallel jurisdictions which are in full communion*

In the context of the provinces of the Catholic Church and running across diocesan boundaries, there can be parochial communities of closely related but culturally distinct churches with distinct practices (e.g. diaspora communities of Eastern Catholic churches). Parallel and overlapping jurisdictions coexist in a structured way. Anglicans may find here a useful model in which culturally distinct parallel jurisdictions exist but with relationships of full communion between them.

Though the Lambeth Conference has eschewed parallel jurisdictions, they are now to be found within the Anglican Communion. The Catholic tradition may offer ecclesial models in which to place parallel jurisdictions but only on the premise of full communion between them.

99.

Receptive learning about lay involvement in Roman Catholic governance

The Roman Catholic Church could learn from the mandatory roles accorded to the laity in Anglican parochial and diocesan structures, in ways that would nevertheless preserve the executive roles proper to the parish priest and the bishop.

Canon 129 §2 of the 1983 Code of Canon Law states: 'Lay members of the Christian faithful can cooperate in the exercise of this same power .... according to the norm of the law'.[27]

100. *Anglican learning about habits of whole-church discernment*

The model of Roman Catholic synods that gather for formation, learning, consultation, and discernment offers a helpful potential expansion to the concerns of Anglican diocesan synods. In particular, practices of ecclesial discernment in common could modify the tendency in some Anglican provinces towards an oppositional style of debate when that is not suited to the discernment of teaching, especially in relation to ethics. Also relevant are the diverse ways in which religious congregations, both Anglican and Roman Catholic, form their members in shared spiritual conversation focused on corporate discernment of the truth.[28]

Roman Catholic learning about whole-church decision-making

The Roman Catholic Church could learn from the Anglican practice of including the voices and concerns of the whole parish or diocesan community in the decision-making of the Church. A particular example is the Anglican practice of wide consultation around the selection and appointment of parish priests and bishops.

---

[27] Pope Francis's 'Motu Proprio' *Mitis Iudex Dominus Iesus* (*MIDI*) now allows lay judges to be in a majority on the panel of three judges in a tribunal.

[28] The Rule of St Benedict and the Dominican tradition have given attention to formalizing this in set procedure, and many other religious congregations have analogous distinct practices.

101. *Anglican receptive learning about participation in the greater whole*

Anglicans are faced with the question of commitment to the unity of the Church, both for the local diocesan church and for the wider Communion. A catholic instinct for unity and participation in a greater whole is a deeply embedded value. Where Anglicans find themselves in situations of fragmentation, they may ask what ecclesial learning can be explored in relation to Roman Catholic universal identity.

Roman Catholic receptive learning about the need for open conversation

The quality of Roman Catholic conversation at parochial and diocesan levels could be enriched by learning from Anglican experience of open and sometimes painful debate while the Church is in process of coming to a common mind (*TT* §52).

102. *Anglican receptive learning regarding ministry*

In some provinces, Anglicans have benefited from the *Catholic Directory for Sunday Worship in the Absence of a Priest*, with deacons, lay readers, or designated lay people leading a celebration of the Lord's Day in the form of a Liturgy of the Word, with or without Holy Communion from the reserved sacrament.

A challenge is to preserve not just provincial but Communion-wide standards for the discernment and theological training of deacons and priests in new contexts. What can Anglicans learn from the Catholic Church in this regard?

Roman Catholic receptive learning regarding ministry

While the Commission recognizes that some decisions regarding ministry made by provinces of the Anglican Communion are not open to the Roman Catholic community, others potentially are, e.g. a female diaconate; a fuller implementation of licensed lay pastoral assistants; the priestly ordination of mature married men (*viri probati*); and the authorization of lay people to preach. Given that the lay faithful already exercise their participation in the *tria munera* by ministering to the Christian community, there is reason to suggest an enlarged role for authorized lay ministry,

including the canonical opening
of the ministry of lector to
women.[29]

103. Both traditions face very similar challenges and pastoral problems
in each of the various cultural contexts in which they exist side
by side. Moreover, both employ similar but differentiated structures to meet these challenges. This Commission recommends that
Anglican and Roman Catholic bishops meet regularly to grow in
friendship, to discuss their pastoral realities and so learn from the
other's experience and wisdom. Likewise, we encourage parochial
clergy and groups of laity, such as parish councils, to meet in their
localities to exchange their diverse experiences and explore how
they might each learn from the other in addressing their challenges.

---

[29] The delegates to the 2008 Synod of Bishops on the Word of God asked that the ministries of
lector and acolyte be conferred on both women and men. Proposition 17 'on the ministry of
the word and women' states, 'It is hoped that the ministry of lector be opened also to women,
so that their role as proclaimers of the word may be recognized in the Christian community.'
The proposition passed with 191 votes in favour, 45 opposed, and 3 abstaining.

V. Instruments of Communion at the Regional Levels of Anglican and Roman Catholic Life

As explained in the Co-Chairs' Preface and in §79, this section has three main subsections: V.A describes what currently is the case for each of our traditions concerning the respective instruments of communion which operate at this level; V.B identifies what respective tensions and difficulties are experienced in relation to these instruments of communion at this level; V.C asks what possibilities there might be for transformative receptive learning from the other tradition in relation to these tensions and difficulties. The Commission has chosen to present our structures, our challenges, and our learnings in parallel columns. At times, in order to avoid appearing to equate quite different processes, we use a sequential format, but with those paragraphs on the left-hand side of the page in an Anglican voice, and those on the right-hand side in a Roman Catholic voice.

The need for regional instruments of communion

104. Anglicans and Catholics recognize that the task of maintaining unity in faith and order *within* the local churches requires instruments of communion *among* the local churches at the regional level (see §§71–73). Both our traditions recognize that their respective regional instruments of communion and their decision-making processes, however imperfect, intend nothing less than the well-being of the local churches and their mission.

Regional churches, trans-local ecclesial bodies, and national boundaries

105. For Anglicans, the regional level is defined by Anglican provincial churches, often contiguous with national boundaries though sometimes comprising several nations. Roman Catholic regional instruments of communion, such as episcopal conferences, serve a single nation or multiple nations. In addition, alongside more formal ecclesial structures, there exist in both communions religious communities and societies with missionary or social vocations of significant influence in a region.

The precedent of local synods

106. From the earliest days of the Church, bishops began to consult about matters of importance in regional synods (see *Auth I* §9; *AS* §3). These were not exclusively clerical gatherings.[30] The experience of both of our traditions is that often the decisions of one region affect the bonds of communion at the worldwide/universal level. Consequently, the history of our traditions shows that trans-local oversight aimed at maintaining unity in Christian life and mission necessarily also entails instruments of communion at the worldwide/universal level (see Section VI).

The regional churches and trans-local ecclesial bodies in engagement with culture

107. The principle of subsidiarity points to the utility of instruments of communion between the local and the worldwide/universal levels of the Church. Not every issue touches everyone in the world, and thus not every issue that affects more than one local church requires deliberation at the worldwide/universal level, which exists to treat issues that affect all.[31] Moreover, cultural differences from one region to another can make a uniform determination ill-advised. This is not to say that truth is culturally conditioned; it is to say that the recognition of a truth, or its expression, is affected by cultural conditions, and so requires discernment by instruments of communion that relate to that culture.

V.A The nature and instruments of communion at the regional levels of Anglican and Roman Catholic life

The asymmetry between our traditions

108. We recognize an asymmetry between our traditions at this level. On account of the history and development of provincial churches, Anglicans invest greater ecclesiological significance in the regional level than the Roman Catholic Church currently does. The canon

---

[30] Yves Congar, *Lay People in the Church* (London: Geoffrey Chapman, 1985), pp. 246–50.

[31] The principle of subsidiarity originates within Catholic social teaching and constitutional discourse. It maintains that decisions should be determined at the lowest *appropriate* level. Proper authority is supportive authority such that if a local body, or lower-level authority, is in need then the relevant wider body, or higher-level authority, will assist. See also *AL* §3: 'Each country or region, moreover, can seek solutions better suited to its culture and sensitive to its traditions and local needs.'

law of the Latin Church currently describes the universal Church and the local churches and the relevant structures and procedures pertaining at these levels but gives relatively little attention to the regional level. In current Roman Catholic practice episcopal conferences respond to regional pastoral issues.

The ancient commonality behind our traditions

109. Despite the obvious dissimilarities of our present ecclesial structures and instruments of communion it is not difficult to discern a familial resemblance stemming from common episcopal, primatial, and conciliar traditions that go back not only before the Reformation but to the earliest days of the Church. This ancient commonality is to be borne in mind as we consider both ecclesial learning and the weight we give to our present structural differences in the light of a common faith. At the same time, we note the different attitudes of the two traditions towards the emergence of the nation state.

The development of Anglican and Roman Catholic regional instruments

110. The historical emergence of the regional or provincial churches of the Anglican Communion is linked to the creation and later development of British colonies around the world. (At the same time there were also other patterns that led to the formation of provincial churches, such as the missionary activities of The Episcopal Church in the nineteenth and twentieth centuries.) The later autonomy of the British colonies as distinct countries was accompanied—and sometimes anticipated—by the creation of autonomous postcolonial churches. An important feature of Anglican provincial churches is their juridical autonomy from one another

In some regions, similar patterns of colonialization to those which affected the global expansion of Anglicanism were pursued by Roman Catholic powers. Despite this, for a range of reasons, the Roman Catholic Church has historically been cautious about embracing expressions of church which could be misunderstood as national churches.

Nevertheless, there has always been the provision for regional meetings of bishops. Significantly encouraged by Pope Leo XIII, by the time of the Second Vatican Council there were forty episcopal conferences. These made a significant contribution to the course of the Council, which, in

and the Church of England, in parallel with the political autonomy of the emerging nations of the Commonwealth. At the same time the churches maintain bonds of affection and common legal and parliamentary traditions. With the emergence of autonomous provinces, the significance of the See of Canterbury was enhanced beyond its historic position as the metropolitical see of the southern province of the Church of England. The 'bonds of affection' specifically with the Archbishop of Canterbury were further enhanced by the convocation of the first Lambeth Conference in 1868 in response to questions of mission, unity, faith, and order arising within and among the regional churches.

turn, encouraged their formation in territories that did not already have them, something which was duly mandated by Paul VI in 1966.[32]

In some respects these episcopal conferences represent a return to the ancient model of regional councils/synods. It should be noted, however, that episcopal conferences are distinguished by the fact that they regularly hold plenary sessions, whereas regional councils/synods tended to be convoked on an occasional basis.[33]

Metropolitan provinces also represent a form of trans-local or regional expression of the Church, though their function and competence have not always been clear. Two recent letters 'Motu Proprio' reaffirm the juridical role of the metropolitan bishop, indicating that not all appeals from the local level need recourse to Rome (*MIDI* and *Mitis et misericors Iesus*, 2015).

The competence of Anglican and Roman Catholic regional instruments

111. The instruments of communion within an Anglican province include determinative juridical

The teaching role and authority of episcopal conferences excite keen interest today because

---

[32] See *CD* §§37–38; also Pope Paul VI, *Ecclesiae Sanctae*, Apostolic Letter issued 'Motu Proprio' on Implementing the Following Decrees of Vatican Council II: *Christus Dominus, Presbyterorum Ordinis, Perfectae Caritatis*, and *Ad Gentes Divinitus* (1966), §41.

[33] Although the writings of St Cyprian and St Augustine indicate that synods were a regular matter in North Africa. See Francis A. Sullivan, SJ, 'The Teaching Authority of Episcopal Conferences', *Theological Studies*, 63 (2002), 472–93 (p. 493).

bodies and gatherings in which the bonds of affection are tested and strengthened by mutual consultation and decision-making. Each province gathers clergy and laity in synod (a general synod or convention) with its president (primate, archbishop, presiding bishop, or metropolitan). Synods deliberate on matters of faith and doctrine, liturgy, and order. They also address national and social questions of importance in their cultural and political context. Regional or provincial statements are frequently read beyond their immediate contexts and have a significant global impact.

the bishops of a region inevitably have to wrestle with the doctrinal issues connected to pastoral concerns. However, the precise relationship between the teaching role of these conferences and the teaching role of the individual bishop on the one hand, and the teaching role of the worldwide episcopal college on the other, is still being debated.

Often the pastoral letters of episcopal conferences not only serve the regional church and its particular dioceses but contribute also to the *sense* of the universal Church concerning certain issues. For example, teaching concerning economic justice, the arms race, capital punishment, nuclear power, the doctrine of the eucharist, and other issues has been well served by the reflections of individual episcopal conferences and by the collaboration of representatives of other episcopal conferences. Significant here is the frequency with which Pope Francis references such documents in his post-synodal exhortation *Evangelii Gaudium* and his encyclical letter *Laudato Si'*, thus recognizing their *de facto* authority.[34]

---

[34] Also significant is the fact that c. 753 of the 1983 Code of Canon Law states: 'Although they do not enjoy infallible teaching authority, the bishops in communion with the head and members of the college, whether as individuals or gathered in conferences of bishops or in particular councils, are authentic teachers and instructors of the faith for the faithful entrusted to their care; the faithful must adhere to the authentic teaching of their own bishops with a sense of religious respect.'

Complementing the increasing internal significance of this level of Roman Catholic teaching, the ability to speak with a coordinated voice is essential if the bishops of a given region or country are to be able to engage effectively with the public legislative agenda.

The structure and operation of Anglican and Roman Catholic regional instruments

112. The synod (or equivalent) of a province retains authority over doctrine and worship, and governs ecumenical relationships and operations of the provincial structures. The three houses, bishops, clergy, and laity, share in the deliberations of the synod. Rules governing decision-making vary according to the nature of the resolution presented, with issues of doctrine and worship requiring more stringent levels of agreement in order to be approved. A significant change may require voting at two successive synods with significant majorities (two-thirds or three-quarters) and additional diocesan consultations and/or approvals between the synods. A house of bishops has particular responsibility as no resolution may be enacted without its agreement. Voting separately by orders is in most cases required to ensure that

Episcopal conferences meet in plenary session, annually or more frequently. Standing committees composed of both bishops and others, in some places including laity, carry on the work of the conference between plenary meetings. These standing committees are supported by national offices. Although there may be lay participation in national offices and associated standing committees of the episcopal conferences, none of the synodal structures at the national level involve lay people. While the 1983 Code of Canon Law provides for national synods and pastoral councils, the occurrence of such bodies is currently very rare.

Within the territory of episcopal conferences there are also smaller groupings of dioceses called provinces headed by a metropolitan archbishop. Appeals from diocesan bishops

episcopal oversight is protected (*PCL* §50.5).

The bishops generally have no juridical authority as a body other than when they participate in the synod as a house of bishops. The bishops of a province do, however, also meet for consultation and fellowship. This is a significant forum for discussion of issues facing the province.

or tribunals are made to this level, and not immediately to a higher level, for resolution (*MIDI* §§V, VI).

Means by which regional instruments can seek wider consultation

113. In the past international voluntary societies for mission, education, and fellowship have contributed much to the life of the Anglican Communion. Of major significance today are certain official inter-regional Anglican meetings, such as the Council of Anglican Provinces of Africa (CAPA), which has addressed, for example, issues of justice, peace, and inter-religious dialogue.

Over the last twenty years, in the light of significant disagreement on issues of human sexuality, informal inter-regional gatherings have offered opportunities for consultation. For example, Global South Anglicans have convened consultations of clergy, laity, and bishops for mutual support and doctrinal discernment. Other bishops from North America and Africa have met together annually for

In cases where an issue under consideration has ramifications outside the region of a particular episcopal conference, the same concerns that led to the establishment of episcopal conferences have led to the formation of wider geographical associations, or federations, of episcopal conferences, such as the Latin American Episcopal Council (CELAM), the Federation of Asian Bishops' Conferences (FABC), and the Council of European Bishops' Conferences (CCEE). Wider consultation can also occur on a more ad hoc basis. An example is the meeting of delegates of European Bishops' Conferences with the leadership of the United States Conference of Catholic Bishops during the preparation of the American Bishops' Pastoral Letter on War and Peace in 1983.

consultation with a view to fostering deeper understanding and fellowship.

Another instrument of wider communion is the convocation of a particular regional synod of bishops. Unlike the federations, which foresee the participation of all the bishops of a larger region, a synod consists of a smaller group of elected bishops from each of the episcopal conferences involved, as well as participants from dicasteries[35] of the Roman Curia that are involved in the particular topic under consideration.

Similarly, a further expression of the felt need to ensure that communion within a region expresses communion at a wider level is the practice of periodic *ad limina apostolorum* visits by all the bishops of a region. The bishops make a pilgrimage to the tombs of the apostles and meet the Bishop of Rome and the Roman Curia to share in dialogue about the state of the churches, with all the strengths and weaknesses to be found in them (*Gift* §59).

The role of the primate

114.   The need for a primate within a region has been recognized at least since the fourth century. A function of oversight of the other bishops of their regions was assigned to the bishops of prominent sees (see *Auth I* §§10–12). The Council of Nicaea (325) already speaks of 'metropolitan' bishops (e.g. Canon 4), and Canon 34 of the *Apostolic Constitutions* (circa 350–380) speaks of the *protos* of each region (see *Auth I* §§22–23; *Auth II* §§16–22).

---

[35] The term 'dicastery' is a generic word for all the departments of the Roman Curia, which includes congregations, councils, secretariats, commissions, and other entities known simply by their proper names.

The selection or election of primates, presidents of episcopal conferences, and patriarchs

115. Most national provinces elect a primatial bishop, archbishop, or metropolitan from among the bishops of the region. A few have traditional primatial sees such that the primate is the bishop of that see (e.g. Canterbury, York, Armagh, Dublin, Cape Town). The primate convenes consultations with the house or college of bishops of the region and presides at the general synod or assembly.[36] A standing committee, executive committee, or archbishop's council assists the primate between gatherings of provincial synods.

Within some national provinces of the Communion, clusters of dioceses form an ecclesiastical province with its own provincial synod or convocation.[37] Such provinces have a particular range of responsibilities, which can include discipline and visitation related to the particular ecclesiastical province. A metropolitan bishop is elected or appointed for the province.

While the title of primate survives in the Roman Catholic Church, not every country has one. Where a 'primatial see' is spoken of, it may only mean the oldest Roman Catholic diocese of a region, e.g. Baltimore in the USA. The Roman Catholic Church also retains provinces presided over by metropolitan archbishops. Both primates and metropolitans have, to some extent, been superseded by the newer offices within episcopal conferences.

Canons 451 and 452 of the Latin rite code direct each episcopal conference to draw up its own statutes, to be reviewed by the Apostolic See, and to elect its own president and other officers.

The Eastern churches in communion with the Bishop of Rome are headed by patriarchs or major archbishops. Patriarchs are elected by the synod of bishops of the patriarchal church. Catholic canon law differentiates between the authority of a patriarch within the traditional territory of the patriarchal church and outside it.

---

[36] In some provinces the primates may delegate the chairing of particular sessions to other bishops, clergy, or lay people.

[37] e.g. in Australia, Canada, England, Nigeria, Ireland, and The Episcopal Church (USA). For historic reasons, England and Ireland also have two primates.

V.B Tensions and difficulties in the practice of communion at the regional levels of Anglican and Roman Catholic life

116. *Tensions between synodal processes and the exercise of episcopal authority*

Within the synods of Anglican provinces, the parliamentary inheritance can inhibit the full exercise of the teaching role of the bishops and reduce synods to juridical and practical decision-making bodies. To develop deeper conversations in such discernment, some provinces are exploring complementary consultative processes. Moreover, parliamentary procedures can sometimes obscure the teaching authority of the college of bishops.

The teaching authority and competence of episcopal conferences

The Roman Catholic Church struggles to articulate a formal theological basis for the nature and extent of the teaching authority of episcopal conferences in relation to the ordinary (non-defining) teaching magisterium of the Church.[38] Currently there is a need to identify more clearly the range and type of issues which properly fall within the remit of national and regional episcopal conferences without direct recourse to Rome.[39]

117. *The potential for division posed by provincial autonomy*

Provincial autonomy gives the provinces of the Anglican Communion the freedom to determine doctrinal expression, liturgy, and canon law. However, the autonomy of provinces can leave them susceptible to cultural and political pressure in

A centralized structure challenges appropriate attention to regional, inculturated experience

The centralized nature of Roman Catholic polity presents challenges to the expression of Catholic teaching and practice being effectively articulated in a way that reflects the perceptions

---

[38] See Pope Francis, *EG* §32: 'The Second Vatican Council stated that, like the ancient patriarchal Churches, episcopal conferences are in a position "to contribute in many and fruitful ways to the concrete realization of the collegial spirit" [*LG* §23]. Yet this desire has not been fully realized, since a juridical status of episcopal conferences which would see them as subjects of specific attributions, including genuine doctrinal authority, has not yet been sufficiently elaborated. Excessive centralization, rather than proving helpful, complicates the Church's life and her missionary outreach.' The penultimate sentence references *AS*.

[39] See *AS* §15. While stating that it is not possible to give an 'exhaustive list' of issues that fall under the competence of episcopal conferences, Pope John Paul II nonetheless here lists thirteen such issues, ranging from the promotion and safeguarding of faith and morals to the use of means of social communication.

local contexts which may strain communion at the global level. While this may be appropriate for mission in the local context, it can sometimes put the province at variance with the wider Anglican Communion and ecumenical partners.

and concerns of the diverse local churches throughout the world.

This tension not only reflects difficulties which can arise when inculturating Catholic teaching. It also reflects the difficulties that regional episcopal colleges experience in having their proposals ratified by the universal Church.

118. *Selection processes can lead to a lack of expertise*
The lack of clear criteria and procedures in some provinces for the election or the nomination of representatives to provincial bodies can lead to imbalances or lack of expertise. This can reduce the capacity of such bodies for informed discernment and decision-making (see §122).

The lack of fora involving priest, deacons, and laity at the regional level
Bishops' conferences have a permanent secretariat and a number of commissions and offices employed to carry out the work of the conferences, which are typically staffed by priests and lay people. Beyond such employees and nominated consultors to the conference, priests, deacons and laity have a limited role in considerations at the national/regional level.

V.C Potential receptive ecclesial learning at the regional levels of Anglican and Roman Catholic life

119. Despite the noticeable asymmetry between Anglican and Roman Catholic structures at the regional level, their very differences represent possibilities for receptive ecclesial learning.

120. *Learning to listen to the wider communion*
The Roman Catholic ethos of belonging to one family could offer the principle of the presence of a voice from outside the province representing the wider

Learning to strengthen the role of regional instruments
As the Roman Catholic Church seeks to strengthen the role of the regional levels of its life, Catholics could profit from asking what there is to be

Church in the deliberations and life of a regional church. This has been recognized in the partners in mission programmes among the churches of the Anglican Communion. It could offer support, receptive learning, mutual understanding, and witness to the communion with the wider Church through the See of Canterbury. The Roman Catholic practice of the presence of an Apostolic Nuncio offers parallels.[40] However, a comparable Anglican role, appointed by the Archbishop of Canterbury or Secretary General of the Anglican Communion, would not be invested with the same juridical authority in relation to the See of Canterbury.[41] In addition to the widespread practice of diocesan twinning, other models of mutual visitation could be profitably developed. This would not only strengthen of the bonds of affection but also be an instrument of effective communion between different centres of the Anglican Communion.

learned from the characteristic theology and associated principles of the provincial church in Anglican tradition.

The stronger authority of Anglican regional instruments of communion, and their greater potential for a pastoral response to local cultures and circumstance, suggests a way in which the teaching role of Roman Catholic episcopal conferences could be strengthened. What might be called a 'pastoral magisterium', the pastoral development of teaching that is formulated in a more abstract manner at the universal level, is a role suggested by the apostolic exhortation *Amoris Lætitia*. There Pope Francis writes, 'Different communities will have to devise more practical and effective initiatives that respect both the Church's teaching and local problems and needs' (*AL* §199). He also states, 'Each country or region, moreover, can seek solutions better suited to its culture and sensitive to its traditions and local needs' (*AL* §3).[42]

---

[40] Following the murder of Bishop Janani Luwum in Uganda, Anglican bishops in Uganda were grateful for both the support of local Catholic bishops and the presence of the Apostolic Nuncio, who provided an essential connection to the wider world in a time of oppression and fear, supporting the work of Bishop Leslie Brown.

[41] After LC 2008 churches were asked to consider inviting two pastoral visitors to reflect upon the issues being discussed, particularly in relation to decisions concerning human sexuality.

[42] Also 'It is up to the Christian communities to analyse with objectivity the situation which is proper to their own country, to shed on it the light of the Gospel's unalterable words and to draw principles of reflection, norms of judgment and directives for action from the social teaching of the Church.' Pope Paul VI, *OA* §4.

121. *Anglican learning about corporate episcopal leadership*
The emerging patterns of Roman Catholic episcopal conferences offer alternative ways for corporate episcopal leadership to be exercised at a provincial level. The development of the corporate sense of episcopacy at the regional level can be seen as more flexible in its response to immediate needs and aspirations than the holding of occasional synods.

The inherent governing and teaching role of the college of bishops of each province could be strengthened, without diminishment of the proper synodical role of clergy and laity. This is particularly the case in respect of the teaching role of all bishops. In the UK a specific example is afforded by the widely appreciated statement issued in 1996 by the Catholic Bishops' Conference of England and Wales, *The Common Good.*

Catholic learning about theological and juridical principles
The potential for learning from Anglican polity and procedure in relation to the provincial level is particularly strong in relation to the Roman Catholic need to develop principles concerning:
– the authority of bishops' conferences;
– the relationship between national/regional bishops' conferences and the Synod of Bishops;
– the identification of the range and type of issues that can be properly dealt with at the local level without routine recourse to Rome;
– appropriate means by which national/regional bishops' conferences might question initiatives and directives emanating from Rome.

122. *The appointment of consultors*
When there are identified gaps of expertise or imbalances in some Anglican provincial synods, a remedy might be learning from the regular Roman Catholic practice of appointing consultors—lay and ordained—to the committees of episcopal conferences (as is already the case in some provinces of the Anglican Communion).

The establishment of synodal bodies at a national level involving lay and ordained
For the Roman Catholic Church to discern right teaching, opportunities for discernment and discussion are always needed at a variety of levels. Such discussion can inform the bishops as the authoritative teachers of the faith. If laity, religious, and clergy are to make a stronger

and more prominent contribution to this process, then it may be fruitful periodically to implement the canonical provision for regional and, perhaps, even national synodal bodies which include laity, religious, and clergy (*CIC* c. 439). While recognizing that no straightforward transfer is possible, the Anglican tradition nevertheless offers useful models as to how such bodies might operate.

Further, given the ways in which the executive role of bishops is generally protected in the Anglican tradition while according a deliberative role to laity and clergy (see *Gift* §39), it is likewise conceivable that laity, religious, and clergy could be given a deliberative vote in Roman Catholic provincial/regional councils on many matters of worship, pastoral outreach, community self-discipline, etc. which follow from tenets of faith and morals (i.e. *fides et mores*).

VI. Instruments of Communion at the Worldwide/Universal Level of Anglican and Roman Catholic Life

As explained in the Co-Chairs' Preface and in §79, this section has three main subsections: VI.A describes what currently is the case for each of our traditions concerning the respective instruments of communion which operate at this level; V.IB identifies what respective tensions and difficulties are experienced in relation to these instruments of communion at this level; VI.C asks what possibilities there might be for transformative receptive learning from the other tradition in relation to these tensions and difficulties. The Commission has chosen to present our structures, our challenges, and our learnings in parallel columns. At times, in order to avoid appearing to equate quite different processes, we use a sequential format, but with those paragraphs on the left-hand side of the page in an Anglican voice, and those on the right-hand side in a Roman Catholic voice.

The shared inheritance of universal instruments of communion

123.   The 'ancient common traditions' that Anglicans and Catholics share include a common recognition of the service rendered by instruments of communion at the worldwide level. These instruments include both the great ecumenical councils of the first millennium and the ways in which the Petrine ministry was exercised to support the unity of the Church. Such structures have evolved from New Testament times and continue to be subject to renewal and development under the providence of God (see *Auth I Elucidation* §8; also *Gift* §§45–47). The common tradition was formed and developed with a sense of worldwide mission that necessitated coordination of efforts.

Now, however, there are significant differences. The Anglican stress on the significance of provinces has led to the development of regional structures in the service of communion. Anglicans are concerned to ensure that the provinces remain doctrinally cohesive despite great diversity of ecclesial life. In order to promote such cohesion, Anglican provinces have developed instruments of communion at the worldwide level. These tend to rely on bonds of affection and self-discipline rather than on binding norms for their implementation. Catholics, especially since regional gatherings of bishops became infrequent in the early modern period, have stressed the universal instruments of communion, arguably to the detriment of regional ones.

Respective self-understanding relative to the one, holy, catholic, and apostolic Church of Christ

124. Anglicans identify the 'one, holy, catholic, and apostolic church' as genuinely visible, realized, and instantiated, albeit imperfectly, in current churches, with ongoing dialogue and ecumenical partnerships drawing the churches towards the full visible manifestation of the Church.[43]

The Lambeth Conference since 1888 has endorsed the Lambeth Quadrilateral as expressing a fundamental Anglican principle. Its intention is to formulate the necessary elements for unity between Anglican and other churches: the Holy Scriptures as containing all things necessary for salvation; the Apostles' Creed and the Nicene Creed as sufficient statements of faith; the dominical sacraments of baptism and the eucharist; and the 'historic episcopate'. While the Quadrilateral has been nuanced

At the Second Vatican Council the Roman Catholic Church moved from articulating its relationship with the one, holy, catholic, apostolic Church of Christ in terms of strict and exclusive identity to stating that the Church of Christ 'subsists in' (*subsistit in*) the Roman Catholic Church (*LG* §8). Read within the canon of Second Vatican Council texts, four significant claims can be found here:

a) nothing essential to the Church of Christ (in terms of unity, holiness, catholicity, and apostolicity) is lacking in the Roman Catholic Church (*UR* §3);

b) the Church of Christ is not to be found in perfect, eschatologically completed form in the Roman Catholic Church, which is itself in need of continual reformation (*UR* §6) and purification (*LG* §8);

---

[43] See 'The Anglican Communion has never seen its life as a family of Churches as self-sufficient, nor does it claim any universal identity other than as part of the One Holy Catholic and Apostolic Church.' LC 2008, Lambeth Conference Resolutions. Section E: Ecumenism, §71. The Declaration of Assent made by those being ordained (or moving to new office) in some provinces includes a solemn assent that the relevant Anglican provincial church 'is part *of the One, Holy, Catholic and Apostolic Church* ...'.

and reinterpreted over the years, its four elements have become fundamental for Anglican ecclesiological identity.

c) nor is the Church of Christ coextensive with the boundaries of the Roman Catholic Church: key elements are to be found within the other traditions (see *LG* §8 and *UR* §3; see *UUS* §11), sometimes even in more developed form—in fuller flower, as it were—than has been the case within the Roman Catholic Church as it currently exists;[44]

d) current ecclesial divisions also diminish the Roman Catholic Church (see *UR* §4): consequently, each tradition has much to learn and receive as we journey towards a reconciled Church that can at once be a more effective sacrament of and witness to the communion of the Trinity (see *UR* §4).

VI.A The nature and instruments of communion at the worldwide levels of Anglican and Roman Catholic life

125. The Anglican Communion continues to discern how best to support its unity with the aid of appropriate structures. Over the last 150 years, four instruments of communion have emerged to give shape to that communion as the autonomous churches emerged through a process of

The universal communion of the local churches is primarily expressed in the communion of the bishops of these churches: 'Just as in the Gospel, the Lord so disposing, St Peter and the other apostles constitute one apostolic college, so in a similar way the Roman Pontiff, the successor of

---

[44] See Pope John Paul II's description, in *UUS* §14, of other Christian communities as places 'where certain features of the Christian mystery have at times been more effectively emphasized'; and *UUS* §48; see also *UR* §§4, 17.

historical, political, and ecclesial devolution. These instruments are: the Lambeth Conference, the Archbishop of Canterbury, the Anglican Consultative Council, and the Primates' Meeting.

Although the roles of the various Instruments of Communion have evolved in response to historical developments, they do embody essential principles of ecclesiastical polity.[45]

At the heart of the role of each instrument are relationships, with each other and the whole Communion, rooted first and foremost in a relationship with God in Christ.[46] Consequently, a willingness to meet together for prayer, worship, and dialogue in the context of all being called to share in the mission of God in the world is essential to each.

Peter, and the bishops, the successors of the apostles, are joined together' (*LG* §22; also §8).

A Church council is the fullest manifestation of the episcopal college. The Bishop of Rome is head of the college and can act on behalf of the whole. The Roman Curia assists him in service of the universal communion of the Church. Synods of bishops are occasional and partial manifestations of the college. Although Roman Catholic documents do not enumerate only four instruments of communion, the Commission identifies these four recognized instruments because they can be examined in a manner comparable to Anglican structures.

It should be remembered that many of the particular structures that facilitate the collegial ministry of the bishops have not been given to the Church by dominical command and are therefore mutable and reformable.

The character of decisions made at the universal level

126. Decisions made by the instruments of communion at the worldwide level are non-binding on the provinces and have authority only when they are received and implemented.

Two of the instruments of communion that operate at the universal level—ecumenical councils and the Bishop of Rome as head of the episcopal college—can definitively declare

---

[45] IASCUFO *Report*, §1.24; see also *VR* §§6.34–6.35; and *WR* sect. C, §§97–104; §§118–20.

[46] It is for this reason that the IASCUFO *Report* refers to them as '... particular ways of facilitating practices that attend to the incarnate Lord and enhance the life of the body of Christ' (§6.4.2).

a revealed truth to be an article of faith, a dogma. Thus, for Catholics, these two universal instruments hold the possibility of definitively resolving theological questions and discerning right teaching. Although authoritative, most magisterial teaching at the universal level is not definitive. Nevertheless, in certain circumstances, the magisterium can resolve matters of faith and morals definitively. In *Mary: Grace and Hope in Christ*, in discussing definitive doctrine, ARCIC II notes: 'Roman Catholics have pointed to the *sensus fidelium*, the liturgical tradition throughout the local churches, and the active support of the Roman Catholic bishops (cf. *Gift* §§29–30): these were the elements through which these doctrines were recognized as belonging to the faith of the Church, and therefore able to be defined (cf. *Gift* §47). For Roman Catholics, it belongs to the office of the Bishop of Rome that he should be able, under strictly limited conditions, to make such a definition (cf. *Pastor Aeternus* [1870], in *Denzinger-Schönmetzer, Enchiridion Symbolorum* [DS] 3069–3070)' (*Mary* §62; see *LG* §25).

Worldwide councils and meetings

127. ARCIC I identified the intertwined origins of primacy and conciliarity.[47] When there was conflict in the early Church, regional
councils, generally convoked by the principal bishop of the region,
came together to discuss and deal with the problems faced by the
churches. Similarly, some wider councils of the whole Church came
to be recognized as ecumenical councils (in particular, Nicaea,
Constantinople, Ephesus, and Chalcedon). Inherent in the life of
the Church is a continuing dynamic of conciliarity and primacy,
no matter what the particular historical or cultural setting of a
church may be. Councils at every level have always sought unanimity. The chronicles of councils show the enormous lengths to
which participants went in order to muster consensus and to avoid
damaging close votes. Furthermore, from the beginning, councils
have proceeded mostly by specifying those positions which are not
compatible with the apostolic faith. Although the condemnation of
a proposition and those who hold that proposition (an *anathema*
or proscription, sometimes denoting excommunication) sounds
draconian to our modern sensibilities, it leaves the door open to
exploration of what is *not* condemned. As such, it is preferable to
an approach which may seem more positive, but which might actu-
ally smother investigation and debate. Councils, therefore, have
primarily taught by judging what is, or is not, consonant with the
apostolic faith, leaving to theologians and others the task of articulating positively that faith.

General Council

128.

The worldwide Roman Catholic
Church has held three coun-
cils since the Reformation: the
Council of Trent (1545–63), the
First Vatican Council (1869–
70), and the Second Vatican
Council (1962–5). Leaving
aside the question of whether

---

[47] See *Auth I* §§8–12 and 19–23; see also '[Though the] declaration and guardianship of the faith
has always been regarded as belonging fundamentally to the episcopal office, the collegiality
of the episcopate must always be seen in the context of the conciliar character of the Church,
involving the *consensus fidelium*, in which the episcopate has its place.' Report of Section III,
'The Renewal of the Church in Unity', in LC 1968, *Resolutions and Reports*, p. 138.

these councils are properly called ecumenical or general, they represent the most solemn exercise of teaching authority in the Roman Catholic Church. These councils also express the inherent and unique teaching authority of the college of bishops when they meet together for this purpose. They also are the highest collegial instance of legislative action.

Synod of Bishops

129.

Pope Paul VI implemented the desire of the Second Vatican Council for a system of synods of bishops. An ordinary synod is convoked every three or four years for treating some aspect of concern to the Church worldwide. Most delegates are elected from episcopal conferences, with larger conferences having more delegates. Heads of dicasteries of the Roman Curia participate, as do representatives of international conferences of major superiors of religious men. The Pope also appoints a small number of non-voting delegates, among them religious women, laity, and ecumenical observers.

Before a synod meets, episcopal conferences are expected to discuss the relevant issues, responding to a questionnaire from the Synod Office in the Vatican. They also may respond to the *Lineamenta* that the Synod Office draws up as an initial response to the conferences' deliberations. There is then some universal input that precedes the deliberations of the synod participants. Lay people are invited to participate in those discussions.

Despite the currently consultative nature of the Synod, provision is made in the Latin Code of Canon Law for the Pope to grant it deliberative power. In such a case, it falls to the Pope to ratify the decisions of the synod (*CIC* c. 343).

Lambeth Conference

130. Successive meetings of the Lambeth Conference have called together bishops from around the globe for consultation and support and to exercise their teaching ministry. These conferences are not intended to exercise judicial responsibility over the provinces through their deliberations or to give the Archbishop of Canterbury authority over any particular provincial or national level. The 1930 Conference described the Anglican Communion as 'a fellowship, within the One Holy Catholic and Apostolic Church, of those duly constituted dioceses, provinces or regional churches in communion with the See of Canterbury' which 'uphold

and propagate the Catholic and Apostolic faith and order as they are generally set forth in the Book of Common Prayer' and which 'are bound together not by a central legislative and executive authority, but by mutual loyalty sustained through the common counsel of the bishops in conference' (LC 1930, §49).

Although not themselves legislative, the conferences carry considerable moral authority and are significant opportunities for episcopal consultation. Their non-juridical resolutions on important issues, such as polygamy and baptismal policy, contraception, matters to do with provincial polity and constitutions, apartheid, human sexuality, and the ordination of women, have frequently formed the basis for subsequent juridical resolutions within the provinces.[48]

Anglican Consultative Council (ACC)

131. The ACC was established by the 1968 Lambeth Conference, as 'a consultative body for the

---

[48] On occasion congresses of Anglicans from across the provinces have gathered for consultation mandated by the Lambeth Conference. There were Anglican congresses in the early years of the second part of the twentieth century. These did not attempt a parliamentary-type synod but involved large numbers of bishops, clergy, and laity from all over the world in a less legislative but highly significant way of 'walking along the road together' (synodality rather than a synod). The most famous of these was held in Toronto in 1963. Its message succinctly epitomized the nature of global Anglican ecclesial relationships: 'Mutual Responsibility and Interdependence in the Body of Christ'. Whatever the political realities, there was here a defining moment in Anglican ecclesiology: autonomous churches were nevertheless to be mutually interdependent rather than independent.

Communion ... [to] attend to matters relevant to the life of the member churches of the Communion'; while it has the authority 'to consult and to make recommendations', it has 'no power of enforcement as such' (*TSI §5.3.3*). It includes the Anglican Communion Office, which is the administrative secretariat serving the worldwide communion.

This instrument incorporates in a triennial meeting the participation of laity, deacons, priests, and bishops representative of each province. It is the body that determines membership in the Anglican Communion. It is responsible for the secretariat of the Anglican Communion; it sets priorities for expenditure, ecumenical dialogues, missions, intra-Anglican projects, and networks; and it assists in coordinating the work of each of the instruments of communion. To facilitate the work of the Council an executive standing committee is formed, which also includes the Archbishop of Canterbury, representatives of the primates, and representatives of the ACC.

Primates' Meeting

132. In 1978 the Lambeth Conference formally instituted periodic meetings of the primates of the Communion to

strengthen interdependence and further consultation. Such meetings had occurred previously on an occasional basis. Like the Lambeth Conference and the ACC, these meetings do not have legislative authority but carry the moral authority of the office of the participants and offer the Archbishop of Canterbury an opportunity for counsel with the primates of the Communion.

Of these meetings the IASCUFO *Report* states: 'The Primates' Meetings, in order to operate as a part of the body of Christ, have to function in relation to the body and encourage a natural reciprocity between their own deliberations and the wisdom of the wider body. In this sense how the Primates conduct their life together becomes a micro example of what it means for Anglicans to live in a godly way in a worldwide fellowship of churches' (§4.6.2).

Primacy

133. The exercise of the authority of the Bishop of Rome within the churches was discussed in *The Gift of Authority*. This has developed and changed over the years, particularly after the definitive split between East and West in 1054. From the beginning, it was recognized that both the successors to Peter as Bishop of Rome and the church itself, as the church of Peter and Paul, had a unique ministry and authority. Many Anglicans recognize the gift that a Petrine ministry, exercised in fidelity to Scripture and Tradition and in service to the Church universal, can be. *The Gift of Authority*

has shown how Anglicans can be open to receiving the exercise of that ministry (§60).

The Bishop of Rome

134.

Because he holds the See of the local church of Rome, which preserves the witness of Peter and Paul, the Bishop of Rome is believed to have a universal primacy. The First Vatican Council taught that the Pope has supreme, immediate, and ordinary jurisdiction throughout the Roman Catholic Church (that is, in all the local churches). The Second Vatican Council inserted that teaching into the context of episcopal collegiality. The Petrine ministry is a service that promotes unity (*UUS* §§24, 88, 94, 97), not a form of domination. Although the Bishop of Rome as universal primate is able to act on his own authority, Roman Catholic tradition limits his 'separate' actions to a few spheres, such as:
- the canonization of saints
- the naming and rare removal of bishops in the Latin Church, and the offering of communion to bishops elected in the Eastern Catholic churches
- the creation of cardinals
- the convening of ecumenical councils
- the convening of synods of bishops and possibly granting them deliberative status

– in exceptionally rare circumstances teaching with the charism of infallibility (*ex cathedra*)
– as chief legislator of the Roman Catholic Church, promulgating universal church law
– appointing members of the Roman Curia

More often, his role is one of coordinating those instruments which serve the unity and mission of the Church, or of the pastor who encourages his flock.

The Archbishop of Canterbury

135. It is important to note that before the first Lambeth Conference, the Archbishop of Canterbury, though Primate of All England, was not a global primate. He was a local archbishop and metropolitan in England. With the quasi-conciliarity of the Lambeth Conference there also emerged the informal role of *primus inter pares* of the Archbishop of Canterbury within the Anglican Communion. This primacy, largely without juridical power, interrelates to all the instruments of communion as they have emerged and as they continue to develop. The Archbishop of Canterbury convokes the Lambeth Conference; he is President of the Anglican Consultative Council (ACC); and he convokes the Primates'

Meetings and chairs the Standing Committee between the primates and the ACC.

Even if there is no juridical embodiment of this primacy, his ministry can also be seen to be the form of personal *episcope* for the Communion: 'Whoever may be the occupant of the office at the time, the ministry of the Archbishop of Canterbury commends itself to the Anglican Communion and to the universal Church as a paradigm of episcopal oversight that is personal and pastoral and that guides, leads and challenges' (*TSI* 3.4.7).

Despite the lack of juridical authority within any province outside the Church of England of the Anglican Communion, or even outside the Southern Ecclesiastical Province of Canterbury in England, the Archbishop is the visible sign of the unity of the Communion. The voice of the Archbishop is listened to by bishops, clergy, and laity across the Communion.

Anglican offices

136. The staff of the Anglican Communion Office serves the mission and unity of the Anglican Communion. The staff of the Archbishop of Canterbury also serves the mission and unity of the Communion with respect to the role of the Archbishop

of Canterbury as the personal focus of the unity of the Communion.

VI.B Tensions and difficulties in the practice of communion at the worldwide/universal levels of Anglican and Roman Catholic life

137. Current controversies in the Anglican Communion have highlighted the inherent tensions between the juridical autonomy of the provinces and the call to interdependence in communion. When the needs of mission in one province lead to changes that are neither understood nor approved by other provinces, there is strain on the bonds of affection and the capacity of the instruments of communion to respond. There is a reluctance among Anglicans to surrender provincial autonomy, particularly when a change in teaching or discipline is widely acknowledged within a given province to be necessary for its mission. This reluctance has been seen in the hesitancy to adopt the Anglican Communion Covenant currently under discussion.[49]

Apostolos Suos §2 states, 'The individual bishops are … the source and foundation of unity in their particular churches.' In other words, the communion of the local churches is first and foremost manifest in the college of bishops. However, relatively little attention is given to this college in terms of canonically required structure and procedure, and so the expressions of collegiality are few.

Another area of difficulty is that posed by the idea of the college of bishops teaching in a binding manner when dispersed around the world (i.e., when not gathered in council) (see *LG* §25). In Pope John Paul II's apostolic letter *Ordinatio Sacerdotalis* and his encyclical *Evangelium Vitae*, appeal is made to such binding teaching (*OS* §4; *EV* §§57, 62). However, there was no act marking the

---

[49] An Anglican Covenant was suggested in The Windsor Report (2004). Work on a potential design began in 2005 as requested by the Joint Standing Committee of the primates and the Anglican Consultative Council, which led to several draft covenant designs that were reviewed by bishops at the 2008 Lambeth Conference and sent for consultation to the Anglican provinces. Further revision led to a final draft being approved by the Joint Standing Committee in November 2009 for distribution to all provinces for their commitment (see §70). The process of provincial commitments is ongoing.

When a threat to unity is perceived, what is desired is an instrument that can either preserve communion or judge whether a difference is, in fact, Church-dividing. A process to deepen communion was introduced at the 2008 Lambeth Conference in the form of the focused listening termed *indaba*.[50] The use of this process has subsequently extended across the Communion and has proved helpful in strengthening bonds of affection and deepening understanding concerning specific pastoral contexts.

explicit consent of the bishops to this supposed binding teaching.[51] As a result, neither the bishops nor the laity can recognize which teachings require assent until they are proclaimed as binding, either by the Pope acting as head of the college or by an ecumenical council.

General Council

138.

With over 2,200 bishops present, the Second Vatican Council was by far the largest Church council ever. For purposes of comparison, the First Vatican Council had just over 700 bishops in attendance. With the number of bishops in the Roman Catholic Church alone now over 5,100, and with the further challenge of language now that Latin has ceased to function as a unifying

---

[50] 'This conference has taken on a new form—the form of *indaba*—based upon an African ideal of purposeful discussion on the common concerns of our shared life. It is a process and a method of engagement as we listen to one another. An indaba acknowledges first and foremost that there are issues that need to be addressed effectively to foster ongoing communal living. It enables every bishop to engage and speak his or her mind and not to privilege the articulate or the powerful.' LC 2008, *Lambeth Conference Resolutions. Section A: Introduction*, §14.

[51] See Congregation for the Doctrine of the Faith, 'Doctrinal Commentary on the Concluding Formula of the *Professio Fidei*' (1998), §9; and Pope John Paul II, *Ad Tuendam Fidem*, Apostolic Letter 'Motu Proprio' (1998), §3.

language, the future practicality of ecumenical councils is a real question. Notwithstanding these logistical difficulties, and given the vital contribution of councils to the life and faith of the Church through the centuries, doing *without* a structure whereby the college of bishops can make definitive judgements is unthinkable. An evolution of the Synod of Bishops may be of assistance in this regard.

Synod of Bishops

139.

Pope Francis's opening address to the Extraordinary Synod of 2014 highlighted some of the tensions expressed to him regarding the exercise of the Synod of Bishops. There may be, and has been, an undue deference among the bishop delegates that stifles candid deliberation.[52]

Even though episcopal conferences are represented by delegates, the constraints of time, as currently structured, mean that most bishops speak in plenary sessions only via prepared texts. Some only submit written speeches for publication. So there is no free-flowing debate in plenary sessions. Together with questions about the constraints of time and the formal nature of interventions,

---

[52] Pope Francis, 'Greeting ... to the Synod Fathers during the First General Congregation of the Third Extraordinary Assembly of the Synod of Bishops' (6 October 2014).

there have been complaints that the published documents of synods have not adequately reflected the concerns of participants.

Many of the issues addressed in the Synod relate to pastoral questions that have direct impact on all the baptized. Although pre-synodal consultation and the resulting *Lineamenta* seek to represent the voice of the faithful, and lay and clerical experts are also appointed to address the Synod, it remains an ongoing challenge to give an adequate hearing to a range of lay opinion.

Lambeth Conference

140. The agreed statements of the Lambeth Conference carry the moral authority of the size and breadth of the Communion but have no juridical force. Tensions arise when some provinces feel conscientiously obliged to depart from their recommendations while others feel bound to uphold them. It harms communion when individual bishops or the bishops of provincial churches decline to attend the Conference.

The gathering of over 900 bishops for intentional dialogue and discussion is costly and challenging. As the number of bishops in the Anglican Communion continues to increase there are inevitable questions about the future format of the Lambeth Conference.

Anglican Consultative Council (ACC)

141. The relationship between the ACC, a legally incorporated and recognized body, and the Lambeth Conference, the Primates' Meeting, and the Standing Committee of the Anglican Communion remains unclear. For example, although the ACC can establish ecumenical dialogues, it is not clear how far its authority extends in the formal reception of ecumenical agreements or other doctrinal concerns, especially in relationship to the teaching authority that properly belongs to the bishops through the Lambeth Conference. In addition, the relationship and responsibilities of the elected representatives of the ACC in terms of accountability to their provincial churches need clarification.

Primates' Meeting

142. The role and authority of the Primates' Meeting have been a source of tension. The provinces of the Communion differ in their willingness to recognize the implied authority of the meeting. Some question whether the primates act in ways consistent with their

advisory capacity, while others would grant the primates a wider juridical and disciplinary authority.

Bishop of Rome and Roman Curia

143.

As head of the college of bishops, the Bishop of Rome, assisted by the Roman Curia, speaks and acts on behalf of the college. His ministry is an expression of the Church universal. However, if (a) consultation and exchange are not maintained, or (b) the collegiality of the bishops is insufficiently expressed, or (c) properly local and regional authority is not respected, then the exercise of this ministry can appear to be one of centralization rather than being genuinely universal. Decision-making can then seem to be at too great a remove from the pastoral reality of the individual local churches.

Decisions regarding liturgical translations have in recent years highlighted the issue of the appropriate level for deciding about local adaptation and inculturation.

Pope Francis has noted a tendency of bishops to defer too readily to Rome rather than to exercise their own proper authority (*EG* §16). The decision-making authority exercised by Rome (particularly in relation to episcopal appointments), and its power to censure, can render both individual bishops and episcopal conferences reticent and constrained in exercising their proper authority in service of the Word and ministry to the people.

Many also ask for greater efficiency and care in the way individual dicasteries of the Roman Curia attend to, serve, and support the college of bishops.

Archbishop of Canterbury

144. The Archbishop of Canterbury is a diocesan bishop, metropolitan, Primate of All England, and the acknowledged *primus inter pares* of the Anglican Communion. This is reflected in the complex process of appointment involving the Crown in England through the Crown Nominations Commission, which includes members drawn from the Diocese of Canterbury, the wider Church of England, and the Anglican Communion.

There is tension among the various roles of the Archbishop (see §64). The Archbishop of Canterbury bears a significant role in the Church of England and consequent state responsibilities in addition to his role in the Anglican Communion. The combination of all these responsibilities is inevitably demanding.

From time to time the Archbishop is asked to intervene in the life of another provincial church despite his lack of juridical authority outside the Church of England. Such interventions or visits can be made by delegation and invitation for the nurture of the province in question.

VI.C Potential receptive ecclesial learning at the worldwide levels of Anglican and Roman Catholic life

145. Despite Anglican hesitancy to modify provincial autonomy, there is a desire for a worldwide identity and commitment that requires deeper expression in the life of the Communion.

Many Anglicans appreciate the commitment to unity within the Roman Catholic Church. They see that deep ethos of unity woven into Roman Catholic life through a variety of common practices from which Anglicans can learn: a common calendar of saints, a common catechism, a common canon law, and a particular exercise of episcopal collegiality.

Given the unifying effect of liturgy, a commitment to the use of at least one common modern eucharistic prayer in local languages would signal Anglican commitment to visible unity. This receptive learning could also be understood as a

The Roman Catholic Church is continuing to grow in its understanding of the proper mutual accountability and a necessary transparency and interrelationship of the college of bishops and the Bishop of Rome as head of the college. While recognizing that Roman Catholic understanding and practice accord a proper executive role to the Bishop of Rome, it would be fruitful to look carefully at the precise ways in which the relationships between the Archbishop of Canterbury and, respectively, the Lambeth Conference, the ACC, and the Primates' Meeting are understood and structured and to ask whether anything might be learned here. One of the chief roles of the Archbishop of Canterbury is to summarize discussions of instruments of communion with a view to articulating consensus, and so to re-receiving of Anglican liturgical tradition, which is rooted in the Book of Common Prayer but which has become increasingly fragmented.

In a similar way, the provision of an approved common catechism would undergird common formation that can strengthen ties within provinces and across the Communion. Further commitment to the Anglican Cycle of Prayer for each bishop and diocese, as a normative element of public worship, would enhance Communion ties.

Anglicans could learn from the further development of canons, or commonly accepted canonical principles. Anglicans throughout the Communion could formally receive *The Principles of Canon Law Common to the Churches of the Anglican Communion.*

Building on the existing Anglican practice of the Lambeth Conference meeting in Canterbury, can Anglicans further explore the role of the See of Canterbury and its cathedral as the seat of the Archbishop as an instrument of communion? For example, the enlargement of the course for new bishops held in Canterbury annually, though not currently mandatory (unlike the course for new Roman Catholic bishops, who must come to

a great extent he is bound by the processes of communal discernment. As Catholics continue to consider their own processes it may be helpful to ask, firstly, what might be learned regarding the open and transparent reporting of processes of discernment, and, secondly, how these processes could bear fruit within formal teaching.

Rome), could provide a further forum for deepening relationships and commitments. Ongoing opportunities for learning could also be offered. Further, how can the churches of the Communion offer stronger support for the Archbishop of Canterbury in his role as *primus inter pares* of the Anglican Communion?

146. In appreciation of the Roman Catholic commitment to episcopal collegiality in discernment, Anglican bishops could learn from the recent synods of Catholic bishops. Given that it is not feasible to hold the Lambeth Conference at a greater frequency than once a decade, the model of smaller, more frequent synods of bishops for the exploration of particular issues with intensive consultation and dialogue could provide additional opportunities for episcopal discernment. The opportunity for deeper theological and pastoral deliberation, with local input and subsequent gatherings for follow-up, would be welcome.

The manner in which Pope Francis listened to and

In light of the difficulties experienced hitherto with the Synod of Bishops, two reforms born of receptive learning from Anglican practice are possible which would render the quality of universal collegiality practised there more effective.

First, Pope Francis's commendation of frank conversation at the Synod[53] raises the question as to whether the quality of synodal conversation and exchange might be enhanced by learning from the Anglican experience of *indaba* at and since Lambeth 2008. This might model a healthy revitalizing of Roman Catholic conversation which would be of relevance to every level of Roman Catholic life.

---

[53] See Pope Francis, 'Greeting … to the Synod Fathers' (6 October 2014): 'One general and basic condition is this: speaking honestly. Let no one say: "I cannot say this, they will think this or this of me …". It is necessary to say with *parrhesia* all that one feels. After the last Consistory (February 2014), in which the family was discussed, a Cardinal wrote to me, saying: what a shame that several Cardinals did not have the courage to say certain things out of respect for the Pope, perhaps believing that the Pope might think something else. This is not good, this is not *synodality*, because it is necessary to say all that, in the Lord, one feels the need to say: without polite deference, without hesitation.'

articulated debate within the Roman Catholic Church, as reflected in the two recent Synods on the Family in *Amoris Lætitia*, has been carefully observed by Anglicans. His encouragement of subsidiarity in the determination of divisive pastoral issues could well be such an area of receptive learning (*AL* §3).

Second, in line with existing canonical provision and again recognizing the need to preserve the executive function of the Bishop of Rome as head of the college of bishops, Anglican models could be drawn upon in order to move the Synod from being a purely consultative body[54] to being a deliberative body, which is foreseen in the Code of Canon Law (see c. 343).

147. The practice of *ad limina* visits of Roman Catholic bishops to Rome for the purposes of mutual consultation and pilgrimage to the tombs of the apostles St Peter and St Paul offers an interesting model. The participation of Anglicans in such *ad limina* has already been proposed in *The Gift of Authority* (§59).

Since Canterbury is the focus of unity of the Anglican Communion, pilgrimage to meet with the Archbishop of Canterbury for prayer and consultation is desirable. Dialogue of bishops with the Archbishop of Canterbury in smaller groupings than that of the Lambeth Conference could further strengthen bonds of communion (see *Gift* §§40, 59). These visits

Pope Francis's appeal[55] that bishops speak boldly and give clear expression to the perceived needs of the Church fits well with both Anglican habits of mutuality of exchange and the formal procedures and structures which support this. It could fruitfully be explored whether this quality of open mutual exchange might be strengthened in Roman Catholic *ad limina* visits. This might include visiting bishops reporting candidly on their pastoral realities and experienced difficulties with aspects of curial policy and action.

---

[54] Currently, the *propositiones* deriving from the Synod are given to the Pope, who in time issues a post-synodal Apostolic Exhortation which, to a greater or lesser extent, represents the *fruit of the propositiones*.

[55] See Pope Francis, 'Address for the Conclusion of the Third Extraordinary General Assembly of the Synod of Bishops' (18 October 2014).

could also be opportunities for further learning for bishops.

148. Anglicans observe with interest the current discussions of curial reform, in particular the interrelationship between episcopal provinces and the Roman Curia, and the Roman Curia and the Synod of Bishops. Even if present definitions of these instruments develop or change, Roman Catholic documents nevertheless do provide clear binding definitions for them, of a sort that Anglicans currently lack in respect to their own instruments of communion. Clearer definitions of the roles, relationships, and competencies of, and among, the Lambeth Conference, the Anglican Consultative Council, the Primates' Meeting, and the Standing Committee are critical.

While Anglicans may not wish to have the juridical authority of Roman Catholic instruments of communion, they can learn from the clarity of recognized processes for the reception of teachings and decisions of the instruments of communion, whether received positively or negatively.

The core Roman Catholic instinct for unity and participation in the greater whole of the universal Church can tend to assume that the entire Church always needs to move as one on all things, with the consequence that even legitimate cultural and regional differences are suppressed. While there are acknowledged tensions within the Anglican Communion, the Roman Catholic Church might fruitfully learn from the Anglican practice of provincial diversity and the associated recognition that on some matters different parts of the Communion can appropriately make different discernments influenced by cultural and contextual appropriateness.

The existence of distinct churches *sui juris*[56] in full communion with the Bishop of Rome with significantly differing liturgical, canonical, and ministerial norms (e.g. concerning clerical celibacy) already provides precedent in this regard. It is also notable that Pope Francis has been encouraging a greater degree

---

[56] *Sui juris* denotes the proper existence of a Church with its own code of canon law, liturgy, patrimony, theological traditions, and spirituality, under the oversight of its own Patriarch or Major Archbishop together with its own synod.

of regional diversity and sub-sidiarity of Roman Catholic decision-making through regional episcopal conferences.

The authority structures of the Anglican Communion make much more modest claims than do parallel Roman Catholic instruments. As a consequence, Anglicans live with judge-ments that are understood to be more provisional, requiring to be tested and discerned by the *sensus fidelium*.

Christians are confronted with new situations in evolving history. They have to discern whether new ways of life are in agreement with the Gospel. The *sensus fidelium* plays an indis-pensable role in this process of discernment.[57] It takes time before the Church comes to a final judgement. The faithful at large, theologians, and bishops all have their respective roles to play. This requires that Catholics live with provisionality, and give latitude to those instruments which cannot give judgements of the highest authority. By their learning to live with teaching that is improvable, space would be given to the testing and discernment of a proposed teaching.

---

[57] See *EG* §§111–34; Pope Francis, Interview with Antonio Spadaro, in *La Civiltà Cattolica*, 3 (2013), 458–9; *SFLC* §§67–80.

149.   As the two communions consider receptive ecclesial learning at
        the worldwide level, the principle of 're-reception' is particularly
        relevant (see *Gift* §§24–25). Where doctrines have developed and
        been taught in ecclesial separation, such as those since the division
        between Eastern and Western Christianity or since the Reformation,
        it is necessary to be attentive and listen to what the other Christian
        communities say of such developments, recognizing the presence
        of the Spirit in other Christians, their churches, and their commu-
        nities (see *SFLC* §§85–86). Even the obvious differences between
        Anglican and Roman Catholic structures at the global level can,
        with attentive listening, lead to the realization that they are diverse
        expressions of a single reality; they are instruments of communion
        developed in support of the Church local, regional, and universal.
        With such a perception comes a new openness to reconciliation,
        learning, and change.

Conclusion

Growing Together into the Fullness of Christ

The Common Declaration of Pope Francis and Archbishop Justin Welby

150. At their meeting for Vespers in San Gregorio al Celio, on 5 October 2016, Pope Francis and Archbishop Justin signed a Common Declaration, which included these words:

> Fifty years ago Pope Paul VI and Archbishop Ramsey took as their inspiration the words of the apostle: 'Forgetting those things which are behind, and reaching forth unto those things which are before, I press towards the mark for the prize of the high calling of God in Christ Jesus' (Phil 3:13–14). Today, 'those things which are behind'—the painful centuries of separation—have been partially healed by fifty years of friendship. ... We have become partners and companions on our pilgrim journey, facing the same difficulties, and strengthening each other by learning to value the gifts which God has given to the other, and to receive them as our own in humility and gratitude.

In quoting St Paul's letter to the Philippians from the first Common Declaration, Pope Francis and Archbishop Justin speak of the need to move from that which lies behind to conversion and reconciliation. In that service, they gave a personal and public example of what it means to walk together penitentially in the way of communion: they shared together in worship and prayer; they exchanged gifts; they shared in teaching; they commissioned nineteen pairs of bishops, Catholic and Anglican, to walk together in fidelity to Christ. This was a living example of two Church leaders with worldwide or universal responsibility commissioning those bishops to walk together in the way of communion in their own regions.

The Commission's work

151. In its work, the Commission has been guided by past Common Declarations of Popes and Archbishops, which have never wavered from the goal of visible unity, and from calling Anglicans and

Catholics to walk together in communion, as they pursue that goal. Following its mandate, the focus of the Commission has been the Church, local, trans-local, and universal, and the way in which church structures support the mission of the Church. The Commission has studied how, from the time of the apostles, such structures were needed in the service of mission, and how from that time they have continued to develop at all levels of the Church's life, as new questions and difficulties have arisen in diverse contexts, including that of our continued separation. Within the Commission the members of each tradition have sought to learn how the experience and structures of the other tradition might help them address their own questions and difficulties.

Instruments of communion and their imperfection

152. The term 'instruments of communion' emerged in Anglican usage. The Commission found that it could also be applied to Roman Catholic structures and procedures. The Commission recognizes that Anglicans and Catholics share a common heritage. Only in the sixteenth century did the structures and procedures of our two traditions break apart, and in many ways they remain similar. These instruments are seen as prompted by the Holy Spirit and as tokens of divine providence. However, they have developed in the course of history and have been influenced in their form as they have sought to meet the challenge of changing circumstances. As such, even when regarded as essential they are also open to reform. The Commission asks how well the respective structures and procedures we have inherited serve as instruments of communion for the mission of the Church today. The Commission also asks what each tradition can learn from the inheritance of the other, and how far each tradition needs to undergo conversion, renewal, and reform. This requires humility and repentance.

Common affirmations concerning the Church local, trans-local, and universal

153. There are significant aspects which both of our traditions affirm, albeit with characteristically differing emphases. Each affirms a fullness of ecclesial reality at the level of the diocese gathered around its bishop, together with a relative autonomy of church at this level. Each also affirms the need for the local churches to be interrelated at the various trans-local levels of province, nation,

region, and worldwide communion. The trans-local organization of the churches is a clear sign that the Church wants to reach out to the human reality in the diversity of cultures, nations, and even continents. The trans-local structuring of churches has a theological and ecclesiological meaning; it is not simply a sociological necessity: it is an expression of the catholicity of the Church. Catholics and Anglicans agree that the People of God, that is, all the baptized as a whole, are endowed with the unfailing instinct for the faith. Therefore, in discerning matters of faith and morals, Catholics and Anglicans must give attention to what the Spirit may be saying in the other tradition before arriving at a definitive conclusion for their own particular tradition.

Tensions between the local and the universal levels of church structures and procedures

154. Moreover, Anglicans and Catholics experience, albeit asymmetrically, that the local and universal dimensions of the Church's life exist in a certain tension with each other. If there is too strong an emphasis on the autonomy of the local (or provincial), bonds of communion at the universal level may become strained or broken, and there may well be insufficient critical distance from the prevailing local culture. In such cases, through its preoccupation with immediate local concerns, a diocese or regional/provincial church can lose awareness of a vital dimension of its identity within the universal mission of God. Equally, too strong an emphasis on the universal risks the Church becoming overly centralized and monolithic in a way that impedes local adaptation for the sake of mission and leads to the proclamation of a Gospel that does not adequately enter into actual cultural realities.

155. In *Ut Unum Sint* §34 Pope John Paul II speaks of the essential role of examination of conscience in ecumenical dialogue: our ecumenical dialogue needs to be a 'dialogue of consciences'. Recognizing that many sins have contributed to our historical divisions, he states that '*Christian unity is possible*, provided that we are humbly conscious of having sinned against unity and are convinced of our need for conversion.' He continues, 'not only personal sins must be forgiven and left behind, but also social sins, which is to say the sinful "structures" themselves which have contributed and can still contribute to the reinforcing of division.' In his address at Vespers

on the occasion of the fiftieth anniversary of the Anglican Centre in Rome, Archbishop Justin Welby, commenting on a daily prayer used at Lambeth Palace, notes:

> *It is a prayer that recognises the past and present, our sin—and yet comes back to God, who calls us to be one, because to be one is the only way to lead a life worthy of the calling to which we have been called. The difficulty which the prayer faces full on is that the habits of the centuries render us comfortable with disunity—even more so when there is the apparatus of dialogue. Dialogue can be an opiate, dulling the pain of separation; or it can be a stimulant, confronting us with the need for repentance and change.[58]*

For Anglicans and Catholics their respective confessional identities—cherishing the role of the local and regional church (Anglican) and placing high priority on the need for ecclesial unity and coherence (Roman Catholic)—are valued as gifts of grace and providence. Nevertheless these identities themselves are not unaffected by sin, as can be seen when the concern for autonomy becomes one of outright independence and when the concern for ecclesial unity and coherence becomes excessive centralized power. Hence there is the need for ecclesial repentance and for reform of our instruments of communion in this respect. The proposals for mutual receptive learning summarized in the paragraphs below are the first step in taking up the vision of a Church fully reconciled.

Mutual receptive learning

156. Through the study of the Church local, trans-local, and universal, the Commission has asked what Anglicans and Catholics could learn from one another to make us better able to walk together in the way of communion. We believe that Anglicans can learn from Roman Catholic structures and procedures which have developed in the service of unity at the trans-local and universal levels. We also believe that Catholics can learn from Anglican structures and procedures which have developed to ensure consultation and deliberation at the local and trans-local levels. In both cases there needs to be a richer understanding of the role of the laity as those

---

[58] Prayer text: Lord Jesus, Who prayed that we might all be one, we pray to you for the unity of Christians, According to your will, According to your means. May your Spirit enable us to experience the suffering caused by division, to see our sin, and to hope beyond all hope.'

who through their baptism participate fully in the threefold office of Christ as prophet, priest, and king.

Roman Catholic receptive learning from Anglicans

157. The discernment of proper teaching, sound governance, and appropriate pastoral care requires a healthy and open conversation in the Church. In the judgement of the Commission, the Roman Catholic Church can learn from the culture of open and frank debate that exists at all levels of the Anglican Communion, evidenced by the *indaba* process, for example. The Anglican practice of granting a deliberative role to synods and of investing authority in regional instruments of communion indicates that the Synod of Bishops could be granted a deliberative role and further suggests the need for the Roman Catholic Church to articulate more clearly the authority of episcopal conferences. Mindful of the participation in the threefold office of Christ of both laity and the ordained, the Catholic Church can fruitfully learn from the inclusion of laity in decision-making structures at every level of Anglican life.

Anglican receptive learning from the Roman Catholic Church

158. Receptive learning for Anglicans from Roman Catholic ecclesial life begins with an appreciation for the depth of commitment to the unity of the universal Church. In the judgement of the Commission, a renewed commitment to this ethos of unity would be strengthened through commitments such as: the use of at least one common, modern eucharistic prayer across the Communion; the provision of an approved common catechism; formal reception of the *Principles of Canon Law Common to the Churches of the Anglican Communion*; further exploration of the role of the See of Canterbury and its cathedral as the seat of the Archbishop as a focus of unity; and the practice of pilgrimage visits by bishops to meet with the Archbishop of Canterbury for prayer and consultation. Receptive learning from Roman Catholic expressions of episcopal leadership would include reflection on: diverse communities in full communion with one another in the same region; models of episcopal consultation and deliberation as seen in episcopal conferences and the Synod of Bishops as recently developed; the normative presence of a voice from outside the province, representing the wider Church in the deliberations and life of a regional church; and

clarity of recognized processes for discernment, communication, and reception of authoritative teachings and decisions.

Receptive learning and the International Anglican–Roman Catholic Commission for Unity and Mission (IARCCUM)

159.   We commend the receptive learning noted above to IARCCUM and to local Anglican–Roman Catholic groups and commissions, meetings of clergy, and occasional joint meetings of bishops.

The link between this statement and the statement on right ethical teaching

160.   The Commission has not undertaken our comparative study of the structures and procedures of our two traditions as an end in itself. We have studied them as structures and procedures which are instruments of communion—which support and promote communion. It is because of the communion in Christ that we already share that we believe we can learn how that communion can be enriched by drawing on the gifts and experience that we see in the other tradition. When, through the Church's mission in new contexts, new questions arise we need to seek out the ways in which they can best be handled. Clearly, this is important for the discernment of right ethical teaching, which takes time. This will be the focus of the next phase of the Commission's work, in accordance with its mandate.

The call to deeper unity at every level of Church life

161.   This has not been the place to speak of the many ways in which Anglicans and Catholics are already partners on our journey. The commissioning of the nineteen pairs of bishops at San Gregorio to walk together in obedience to Christ bears witness to that. Anglicans and Catholics share a rich 'sharing [*koinonia*] in the gospel' (see Phil 1.5). We do not yet, however, share partnership in the eucharist (see 1 Cor 10.16). What we as yet lack drives us on in search for deeper reconciliation and fuller unity at the local, trans-local, and universal levels of the Church. While we do not yet fully share in the eucharist, we are already in a real yet imperfect communion which impels us towards deeper and fuller reconciliation at the local, trans-local, and universal levels of the Church. We are pilgrims together walking on the way of penitence and renewal towards full communion. On this pilgrimage, Paul's exhortation to

the Ephesian church is most apt: 'I ... beg you to lead a life worthy of the calling to which you have been called, with all humility and gentleness, with patience, bearing with one another in love, making every effort to maintain the unity of the Spirit in the bond of peace' (Eph 4.1–3). These characteristics capture the necessary spirit of our ecumenical journey, and offer us a vision of how we are to continue walking together on the way towards full communion.

Bibliography

Alexander, Loveday. 'Mission and Unity in the Acts of the Apostles', in Christoph Ernst, Christopher Hill, Leslie Nathaniel, and Friederike Nüssel (eds.), *Ecclesiology in Mission Perspective: Contributions to the Seventh Theological Conference within the Framework of the Meissen Process of the Church of England and the Evangelical Church in Germany* (Leipzig: Evangelische Verlagsanstalt, 2012)

Anglican Church of Canada, 'The St Michael Report' (May 2005), available at www.anglican.ca/wp-content/uploads/2010/11/StMichaelReport.pdf

Anglican Communion Office, *The Anglican Communion Covenant*, available at: www.anglicancommunion.org/media/99905/The_Anglican_Covenant.pdf

Anglican Consultative Council, *The Principles of Canon Law Common to the Churches of the Anglican Communion* (London: Anglican Communion Office, 2008)

Anglican–Roman Catholic Consultation in the United States, *Agreed Report on the Local/Universal Church* (15 November 1999), available at: https://iarccum.org/doc/?d=153

Archbishop Justin Welby, Homily at Westminster Abbey Evensong Celebrating 50 years of the Anglican Centre in Rome (15 June 2016), available at: www.archbishopofcanterbury.org/articles.php/5737/archbishop-preaches-at-anglican-centre-in-rome-50th-anniversary-service

Archbishop Justin Welby and Pope Francis, 'Commissioning the IARCCUM Bishops' (5 October 2016), San Gregorio al Celio, Rome, available at: www.anglicancommunion.org/media/271340/commissioning-of-iarccum-bishops.pdf

Archbishop Rowan Williams, Address to the Cardinal Willebrands Symposium at the Gregorian University in Rome on 19 November 2009, Pontifical Council for Promoting Christian Unity, *Information Service*, 132/3–4 (2009), 46–50; *One in Christ*, 43 (2009), 154–66; also available at: www.vatican.va/roman_curia/pontifical_councils/chrstuni/angl-comm-docs/rc_pc_chrstuni_doc_20091119_williams-willebrands_en.html

ARCIC I, *Eucharistic Doctrine* (1971), available at: www.vatican.va/roman_curia/pontifical_councils/chrstuni/angl-comm-docs/rc_pc_chrstuni_doc_1971_eucharistic-doctrine_en.html

ARCIC I, *Authority in the Church I* (Venice, 1976), available at: www.vatican.va/roman_curia/pontifical_councils/chrstuni/angl-comm-docs/rc_pc_chrstuni_doc_197609_authority-church-i_en.html

ARCIC I, *Authority in the Church I: Elucidation* (1981), available at: www.vatican.va/roman_curia/pontifical_councils/chrstuni/angl-comm-docs/rc_pc_chrstuni_doc_1981_authority-elucidation-i_en.html

ARCIC I, *Authority in the Church II* (Windsor, 1981), available at: www. vatican.va/roman_curia/pontifical_councils/chrstuni/angl-comm-docs/ rc_pc_chrstuni_doc_1981_authority-church-ii_en.html

ARCIC I, *The Final Report*, in Christopher Hill and Edward Yarnold (eds.), *Anglicans and Roman Catholics: The Search for Unity* (London: SPCK/CTS, 1994)

ARCIC II, *Salvation and the Church* (1987), available at: www.vatican.va/ roman_curia/pontifical_councils/chrstuni/angl-comm-docs/rc_pc_ chrstuni_doc_19860903_salvation-church_en.html

ARCIC II, *Church as Communion* (1991), available at: www.vatican.va/ roman_curia/pontifical_councils/chrstuni/angl-comm-docs/rc_pc_ chrstuni_doc_19900906_church-communion_en.html

ARCIC II, *Life in Christ: Morals, Communion and the Church* (1994), available at: www.vatican.va/roman_curia/pontifical_councils/chrstuni/angl-comm-docs/ rc_pc_chrstuni_doc_19930906_life-in-christ_en.html

ARCIC II, *The Gift of Authority (Authority in the Church III)* (1999), available at: www.vatican.va/roman_curia/pontifical_councils/chrstuni/documents/rc_ pc_chrstuni_doc_12051999_gift-of-autority_en.html

ARCIC II, *Mary: Grace and Hope in Christ* (2005), available at: www.vatican. va/roman_curia/pontifical_councils/chrstuni/angl-comm-docs/rc_ pc_chrstuni_doc_20050516_mary-grace-hope-christ_en.html

ARCIC III, Communiqué Following the First Meeting (Bose, May 2011), available at: www.anglicancommunion.org/media/105248/ARCIC_III_Bose_2011.pdf

Avis, Paul, *Beyond the Reformation: Authority, Primacy and Unity in the Conciliar Tradition* (London and New York: T & T Clark, 2006)

Avis, Paul, *Becoming a Bishop: A Theological Handbook of Episcopal Ministry* (London and New York: T & T Clark, 2015)

Church of England, *Bishops in Communion: Collegiality in Service of the Koinonia of the Church* (London: Church House Publishing, 2000)

Church of England, *Common Worship* (London: Church House Publishing, 2000)

Church of England, *Common Worship: Ordination Services, Study Edition* (London: Church House Publishing, 2007)

Church of England, *Canons of the Church of England*, 7th edn (London: Church House Publishing, 2012), available at: www.churchofengland.org/about-us/ structure/churchlawlegis/canons/canons-7th-edition.aspx

Coleman, Roger (ed.), *Resolutions of the Twelve Lambeth Conferences, 1867–1988* (Toronto: Anglican Book Centre, 1992)

Congregation for the Doctrine of the Faith, *Communionis Notio*. Letter to the Bishops of the Catholic Church on some Aspects of the Church Understood as Communion (1992), available at: www.vatican.va/roman_curia/congregations/ cfaith/documents/rc_con_cfaith_doc_28051992_communionis-notio_en.html

Congregation for the Doctrine of the Faith, 'Doctrinal Commentary on the Concluding Formula of the *Professio Fidei*' (1998), available at: www.vatican. va/roman_curia/congregations/cfaith/documents/rc_con_cfaith_doc_1998_ professio-fidei_en.html

Denaux, Adelbert, Nicholas Sagovsky, and Charles Sherlock (eds.), *Looking Towards a Church Fully Reconciled: The Final Report of the Anglican–Roman Catholic International Commission 1983–2005 (ARCIC II)* (London: SPCK, 2016)

General Synod of the Church of England, 'The Governance of the Church of England and the Anglican Communion' (7 January 2009), GS Misc 910, §2.2, available at: www.churchofengland.org/media/38963/gsmisc910.pdf

Goodhew, David (ed.), *Growth and Decline in the Anglican Communion, 1980 to the Present*, Routledge Contemporary Ecclesiology (Abingdon, Oxon: Routledge, 2017)

Hill, Christopher, and Edward Yarnold (eds.), *Anglicans and Roman Catholics: The Search for Unity* (London: SPCK/CTS, 1994)

Inter-Anglican Standing Commission on Unity, Faith and Order, *Report to ACC-15*, (2012), available at: www.anglicancommunion.org/media/39744/iascufo-complete-report-to-acc.pdf

Inter-Anglican Standing Commission on Unity, Faith and Order, *Towards a Symphony of Instruments: A Historical and Theological Consideration of the Instruments of Communion of the Anglican Communion* (London: Anglican Communion Office, 2015)

Inter-Anglican Theological and Doctrinal Commission, *The Virginia Report* (London: Anglican Consultative Council, 1997), available at: www.anglican-communion.org/media/150889/report-1.pdf

Inter-Anglican Theological and Doctrinal Commission, *Communion, Conflict and Hope: The Kuala Lumpur Report of the Third Inter-Anglican Theological and Doctrinal Commission* (London: Anglican Communion Office, 2008)

International Anglican–Roman Catholic Commission for Unity and Mission, 'Part One: The Achievements of Anglican–Roman Catholic Dialogue', in *Growing Together in Unity and Mission: Building on 40 Years of Anglican–Roman Catholic Dialogue* (London: SPCK, 2007), available at: www.anglicancommunion.org/media/104627/Growing-Together-in-Unity-and-Mission_english.pdf

International Anglican–Roman Catholic Commission for Unity and Mission, *Walking Together: Common Service to the World and Witness to the Gospel* (7 October 2016), available at: www.vatican.va/roman_curia/pontifical_councils/chrstuni/angl-comm-docs/rc_pc_chrstuni_doc_20161007_walking-together_en.html

International Theological Commission, *Theology Today: Perspectives, Principles, and Criteria* (29 November 2011), available at: www.vatican.va/roman_curia/congregations/cfaith/cti_documents/rc_cti_doc_20111129_teologia-oggi_en.html

International Theological Commission, '*Sensus Fidei* in the Life of the Church' (2014), available at: www.vatican.va/roman_curia/congregations/cfaith/cti_documents/rc_cti_20140610_sensus-fidei_en.html#4._Ecumenical_aspects_of_the_sensus_fidei

Joint International Commission for the Theological Dialogue between the Roman Catholic Church and the Orthodox Church, 'Ecclesiological and Canonical

Consequences of the Sacramental Nature of the Church: Ecclesial Communion, Conciliarity, and Authority', *Ravenna* (13 October 2007), available at: www. vatican.va/roman_curia/pontifical_councils/chrstuni/ch_orthodox_docs/ rc_pc_chrstuni_doc_20071013_documento-ravenna_en.html

Joint International Commission for the Theological Dialogue between the Roman Catholic Church and the Orthodox Church, 'Synodality and Primacy during the First Millennium: Towards a Common Understanding in Service to the Unity of the Church', Chieti (21 September 2016), available at: www.vatican. va/roman_curia/pontifical_councils/chrstuni/ch_orthodox_docs/rc_pc_ chrstuni_doc_20160921_sinodality-primacy_en.html

Lambeth Commission on Communion, *The Windsor Report* (London: The Anglican Communion Office, 2004), available at: www.anglicancommunion. org/media/68225/windsor2004full.pdf

Lambeth Conference 1920, Resolution 9, 'An Appeal to All Christian People: Reunion of Christendom', available at: www.anglicancommunion.org/resources/ document-library/lambeth-conference/1920/resolution-9-reunion-of-christen dom?author=Lambeth+Conference&year=1920

Lambeth Conference 1930, *Lambeth Conference Resolutions*, Resolution 49, available at: www.anglicancommunion.org/resources/document-library/ lambeth-conference/1930/resolution-49-the-anglican-communion?author=La mbeth+Conference&year=1930

Lambeth Conference 1968, *Resolutions and Reports* (London and New York: SPCK and Seabury, 1968)

Lambeth Conference 1998, Resolution IV.11, available at: www.anglicancommunion. org/resources/document-library/lambeth-conference/1998/section-iv-called- to-be-one/section-iv11-continuing-churches?author=Lambeth+Conference& year=1998

Lambeth Conference 2008, *Lambeth Conference Resolutions. Section A: Introduction*, §14, available at: www.anglicancommunion.org/resources/ document-library/lambeth-conference/2008/section-a-introduction?author= Lambeth+Conference&year=2008

Lambeth Conference 2008, *Lambeth Conference Resolutions. Section E: Ecumenism*, §71, available at: www.anglicancommunion.org/resources/document-library/ lambeth-conference/2008/section-e-ecumenism?author=Lambeth+Conferenc e&year=2008

Lambeth Quadrilateral, from the Lambeth Conference 1888, Resolution 11, in Roger Coleman (ed.), *Resolutions of the Twelve Lambeth Conferences, 1867–1988* (Toronto: Anglican Book Centre, 1992); also available at: www.angli-cancommunion.org/resources/document-library/lambeth-conference/1888/ resolution-11?author=Lambeth+Conference&year=1888

Murray, Paul D. (ed.), *Receptive Ecumenism and the Call to Catholic Learning: Exploring a Way for Contemporary Ecumenism* (Oxford: Oxford University Press, 2008)

Pope Benedict XVI, *Anglicanorum Coetibus*. Apostolic Constitution Providing for Personal Ordinariates for Anglicans Entering into Full Communion with the

Catholic Church (4 November 2009), available at: http://w2.vatican.va/content/benedict-xvi/en/apost_constitutions/documents/hf_ben-xvi_apc_20091104_anglicanorum-coetibus.html

Pope Benedict XVI and the Archbishop of Canterbury, His Grace Rowan Williams, 'Common Declaration' (23 November 2006), available at: http://w2.vatican.va/content/benedict-xvi/en/speeches/2006/november/documents/hf_ben-xvi_spe_20061123_common-decl.html

Pope Francis, *Evangelii Gaudium*. Apostolic Exhortation on the Proclamation of the Gospel in Today's World (24 November 2013), available at: http://w2.vatican.va/content/francesco/en/apost_exhortations/documents/papa-francesco_esortazione-ap_20131124_evangelii-gaudium.html

Pope Francis, 'General Audience' (22 January 2014), available at: www.vatican.va/holy_father/francesco/audiences/2014/documents/papa-francesco_20140122_udienza-generale_en.html

Pope Francis, Address to His Grace Justin Welby, Archbishop of Canterbury and his Entourage (16 June 2014), available at: https://w2.vatican.va/content/francesco/en/speeches/2014/june/documents/papa-francesco_20140616_arcivescovo-canterbury.html

Pope Francis, 'Greeting of Pope Francis to the Synod Fathers during the First General Congregation of the Third Extraordinary Assembly of the Synod of Bishops' (6 October 2014), available at: http://w2.vatican.va/content/francesco/en/speeches/2014/october/documents/papa-francesco_20141006_padri-sino-dali.html

Pope Francis, 'Address for the Conclusion of the Third Extraordinary General Assembly of the Synod of Bishops' (18 October 2014), available at: http://w2.vatican.va/content/francesco/en/speeches/2014/october/documents/papa-francesco_20141018_conclusione-sinodo-dei-vescovi.html

Pope Francis, 'Greeting of the Holy Father to Cardinals Gathered for the Consistory' (12 February 2015), available at: http://w2.vatican.va/content/francesco/en/speeches/2015/february/documents/papa-francesco_20150212_saluto-concistoro-cardinali.html

Pope Francis, 'General Audience' (18 February 2015), available at: http://w2.vatican.va/content/francesco/en/audiences/2015/documents/papa-francesco_20150218_udienza-generale.html

Pope Francis, Address to Members of the Anglican–Roman Catholic International Commission (30 April 2015), available at: https://w2.vatican.va/content/francesco/en/speeches/2015/april/documents/papa-francesco_20150430_commissione-internazionale-anglicana-cattolica.html

Pope Francis, *Mitis Iudex Dominus Iesus*. Apostolic Letter 'Motu Proprio' by which the Canons of the Code of Canon Law Pertaining to Cases Regarding the Nullity of Marriage are Reformed (2015), available at: https://w2.vatican.va/content/francesco/en/motu_proprio/documents/papa-francesco-motu-proprio_20150815_mitis-iudex-dominus-iesus.html

Pope Francis, Address Commemorating the 50th Anniversary of the Institution of the Synod of Bishops (17 October 2015), available at: http://w2.vatican.va/

content/francesco/en/speeches/2015/october/documents/papa-francesco_20151017_50-anniversario-sinodo.html

Pope Francis, *Amoris Lætitia*. Post-Synodal Apostolic Exhortation on Love in the Family (2016), available at: http://w2.vatican.va/content/francesco/en/apost_exhortations/documents/papa-francesco_esortazione-ap_20160319_amoris-laetitia.html

Pope Francis and His Grace Justin Welby, Archbishop of Canterbury, 'Common Declaration' (5 October 2016), available at: www.anglicannews.org/news/2016/10/common-declaration-of-pope-francis-and-archbishop-justin-welby.aspx and www.vatican.va/roman_curia/pontifical_councils/chrstuni/angl-comm-docs/rc_pc_chrstuni_doc_20161005_dichiarazione-comune_en.html

Pope John Paul II, Address to ARCIC I (Castelgandolfo, 4 September 1980), available at: https://w2.vatican.va/content/john-paul-ii/en/speeches/1980/september/documents/hf_jp-ii_spe_19800904_cattolici-anglicani.html

Pope John Paul II, *Codex Iuris Canonici*. The Code of Canon Law for Latin Rite Catholic Churches (1983), available at: www.vatican.va/archive/ENG1104/_INDEX.HTM

Pope John Paul II, *Christifideles Laici*. Apostolic Exhortation on the Vocation and the Mission of the Lay Faithful in the Church and the World (30 December 1988), available at: http://w2.vatican.va/content/john-paul-ii/en/apost_exhortations/documents/hf_jp-ii_exh_30121988_christifideles-laici.html

Pope John Paul II, *Pastor Bonus*. Apostolic Constitution (1988), available at: http://w2.vatican.va/content/john-paul-ii/en/apost_constitutions/documents/hf_jp-ii_apc_19880628_pastor-bonus.html

Pope John Paul II, *Codex Canonum Ecclesiarum Orientalium*. The Code of Canons of the Eastern Churches (18 October 1990), available at: http://w2.vatican.va/content/john-paul-ii/la/apost_constitutions/documents/hf_jp-ii_apc_19901018_index-codex-can-eccl-orient.html

Pope John Paul II, *Ordinatio Sacerdotalis*. Apostolic Letter on Reserving Priestly Ordination to Men Alone (1994), available at: https://w2.vatican.va/content/john-paul-ii/en/apost_letters/1994/documents/hf_jp-ii_apl_19940522_ordinatio-sacerdotalis.html

Pope John Paul II, *Evangelium Vitae*. Encyclical Letter on the Value and Inviolability of Human Life (1995), available at: http://w2.vatican.va/content/john-paul-ii/en/encyclicals/documents/hf_jp-ii_enc_25031995_evangelium-vitae.html

Pope John Paul II, *Ut Unum Sint*. Encyclical on Commitment to Ecumenism (1995), available at: http://w2.vatican.va/content/john-paul-ii/en/encyclicals/documents/hf_jp-ii_enc_25051995_ut-unum-sint.html

Pope John Paul II, *Ad Tuendam Fidem*. Apostolic Letter 'Motu Proprio' (1998), available at: http://w2.vatican.va/content/john-paul-ii/en/motu_proprio/documents/hf_jp-ii_motu-proprio_30061998_ad-tuendam-fidem.html

Pope John Paul II, *Apostolos Suos*. Apostolic Letter issued 'Motu Proprio' on the Theological and Juridical Nature of Episcopal Conferences (1998), available at:

http://w2.vatican.va/content/john-paul-ii/en/motu_proprio/documents/hf_jp-ii_motu-proprio_22071998_apostolos-suos.html

Pope John Paul II and Archbishop Robert Runcie, 'Common Declaration' (2 October 1989), in *One in Hope: Documents of the Visit of the Most Reverend Robert Runcie, Archbishop of Canterbury to His Holiness Pope John Paul II, Bishop of Rome* (London: Church House Publishing and Catholic Truth Society, 1989); also available at: http://w2.vatican.va/content/john-paul-ii/en/speeches/1989/october/documents/hf_jp-ii_spe_19891002_dichiaraz-comune.html

Pope Paul VI, *Ecclesiae Sanctae*. Apostolic Letter issued 'Motu Proprio' on Implementing the Following Decrees of Vatican Council II: *Christus Dominus, Presbyterorum Ordinis, Perfectae Caritatis*, and *Ad Gentes Divinitus* (1966), available at: https://w2.vatican.va/content/paul-vi/en/motu_proprio/documents/hf_p-vi_motu-proprio_19660806_ecclesiae-sanctae.html

Pope Paul VI, *Octogesima Adveniens*. Apostolic Letter on the Occasion of the Eightieth Anniversary of the Encyclical *Rerum Novarum* (1971), available at: http://w2.vatican.va/content/paul-vi/en/apost_letters/documents/hf_p-vi_apl_19710514_octogesima-adveniens.html

Pope Paul VI and Archbishop Donald Coggan, 'Common Declaration' (27 April 1977), in *Pilgrim for Unity, Common Declaration between the Most Reverend Donald Coggan, Archbishop of Canterbury and His Holiness Pope Paul VI* (London: SPCK and Catholic Truth Society, 1977), also available at: http://w2.vatican.va/content/paul-vi/en/speeches/1977/april/documents/hf_p-vi_spe_19770429_dichiarazione-comune.html

Second Anglican Encounter in the South, *Kuala Lumpur Report*, §§11b and 12, available at: www.churchsociety.org/issues_new/communion/ctexts/iss_communion_ctexts_kualalumpur.asp

Second Vatican Council, *Sacrosanctum Concilium*. Constitution on the Sacred Liturgy (4 December 1963), available at: www.vatican.va/archive/hist_councils/ii_vatican_council/documents/vat-ii_const_19631204_sacrosanctum-concilium_en.html

Second Vatican Council, *Lumen Gentium*. The Dogmatic Constitution on the Church (21 November 1964), available at: www.vatican.va/archive/hist_councils/ii_vatican_council/documents/vat-ii_const_19641121_lumen-gentium_en.html

Second Vatican Council, *Unitatis Redintegratio*. Decree on Ecumenism (21 November 1964), available at: www.vatican.va/archive/hist_councils/ii_vatican_council/documents/vat-ii_decree_19641121_unitatis-redintegratio_en.html

Second Vatican Council, *Christus Dominus*. Decree Concerning the Pastoral Office of Bishops in the Church (28 October 1965), available at: www.vatican.va/archive/hist_councils/ii_vatican_council/documents/vat-ii_decree_19651028_christus-dominus_en.html

Second Vatican Council, *Apostolicam Actuositatem*. Decree on the Apostolate of the Laity (18 November 1965), available at: www.vatican.va/archive/hist_councils/ii_vatican_council/documents/vat-ii_decree_19651118_apostolicam-actuositatem_en.html

Second Vatican Council, *Ad Gentes*. Decree on the Mission Activity of the Church

(7 December 1965), available at: www.vatican.va/archive/hist_councils/ ii_vatican_council/documents/vat-ii_decree_19651207_ad-gentes_en.html

Second Vatican Council, *Presbyterorum Ordinis*. Decree on the Ministry and Life of Priests (7 December 1965), available at: www.vatican.va/archive/ hist_councils/ii_vatican_council/documents/vat-ii_decree_19651207_ presbyterorum-ordinis_en.html

Toronto Anglican Congress, 'Mutual Responsibility and Interdependence in the Body of Christ' (1963), available at: http://anglicanhistory.org/canada/ toronto_mutual1963.html

United States Conference of Catholic Bishops, 'Summary', in *The Challenge of Peace: God's Promise and Our Response*. A Pastoral Letter on War and Peace (3 May 1983), available at: www.usccb.org/upload/challenge-peace-gods-promise-our-response-1983.pdf

World Council of Churches, *The Church: Towards a Common Vision*. Faith and Order Paper No. 214 (Geneva: WCC Publications, 2013)

World Council of Churches Assembly, *Called to Be the One Church* (Porto Alegre, 2006), available at: www.oikoumene.org/en/resources/documents/ commissions/faith-and-order/i-unity-the-church-and-its-mission/ called-to-be-the-one-church-the-porto-alegre-ecclesiology-text

Yarnold, Edward (ed.), *They are in Earnest* (London: St Paul Publications, 1982)

Members of the Commission

Anglican members

Co-Chair

The Most Revd Sir David Moxon, Archbishop of Canterbury's Representative to the Holy See

Members

Dr Paula Gooder, Canon Theologian, Birmingham Cathedral, Church of England

The Rt Revd Dr Christopher Hill, President of the Conference of European Churches, Church of England

The Revd Canon Professor Mark McIntosh, Durham University, UK (2011–14)

The Rt Revd Nkosinathi Ndwandwe, Suffragan Bishop of Natal, The Anglican Church of Southern Africa

The Rt Revd Linda Nicholls, Bishop of Huron, The Anglican Church of Canada

The Revd Canon Dr Michael Poon, Trinity Theological College, Singapore

The Revd Canon Dr Nicholas Sagovsky, Visiting Professor, King's College London, Church of England

The Revd Canon Dr Peter Sedgwick, formerly Principal, St Michael's College, Llandaff, Church in Wales

Consultant

The Revd Dr Charles Sherlock, Anglican Diocese of Bendigo, The Anglican Church of Australia

Co-Secretary

The Revd Canon Alyson Barnett-Cowan, Anglican Communion Office (2011–14)

The Revd Canon Dr John Gibaut, Anglican Communion Office (2015–present)

Staff

The Revd Canon Jonathan Goodall, Representative of the Archbishop of Canterbury (2011–13)

The Revd Dr William Adam, Representative of the Archbishop of Canterbury (2017–present)

The Revd Neil Vigers, Anglican Communion Office

Roman Catholic members

Co-Chair

The Most Revd Bernard Longley, Archbishop of Birmingham, UK

Members

The Revd Robert Christian, OP, St Albert Priory, Oakland, California, USA

The Revd Canon Adelbert Denaux, Professor Em., Katholieke Universiteit, Leuven, Belgium

The Most Revd Arthur Kennedy, Auxiliary Bishop of Boston, USA

Professor Paul D. Murray, Durham University, UK

Professor Sister Teresa Okure, First Scholar-in Residence, SHCJ Catholic Institute of West Africa, Nigeria

Professor Janet E. Smith, Sacred Heart Major Seminary, Detroit, Michigan, USA

The Revd Professor Vimal Tirimanna, CSsR, Alphonsianum University, Rome, Italy

The Very Revd Dom Henry Wansbrough, OSB, Ampleforth Abbey, UK

Consultants

The Very Revd Dr Peter Galadza, Saint Paul University, Ottawa, Canada

The Revd Father Norman Tanner, SJ, Pontifical Gregorian University, Rome, Italy

Co-Secretary

The Revd Monsignor Mark Langham (2011–13)

The Revd Anthony Currer, Pontifical Council for Promoting Christian Unity (2013–present)

World Council of Churches Observer

The Revd Dr Odair Pedroso Mateus